The Making of
Lewis Carroll's
Alice
and the
Invention of
Wonderland

The Making of
Lewis Carroll's
Alice

and the Invention of Wonderland

PETER HUNT

Bodleian Library
UNIVERSITY OF OXFORD

First published in 2020 by the Bodleian Library
Broad Street, Oxford OX1 3BG
www.bodleianshop.co.uk

ISBN: 978 1 85124 532 1

Text © Peter Hunt 2020

All images, unless specified on p. 127, © Bodleian Library, University of Oxford, 2020

Peter Hunt has asserted his right to be identified as the author of this Work.

Cover design by Dot Little at the Bodleian Library
Designed and typeset by Laura Parker in 9.8 on 15.8 Andulka Pro
Printed and bound through South Sea Global Services Limited
on 157gsm Golden Sun Matt Art paper

MIX
Paper from
responsible sources
FSC® C122901

British Library Catalogue in Publishing Data
A CIP record of this publication is available from the British Library

CONTENTS

CHARLES AND LEWIS

'With a name like yours, you might be any shape, almost'

Most writers about Charles Lutwidge Dodgson and the 'Alice' books choose to call the author by his pen name, 'Lewis Carroll'. He had adopted it in 1856, at the behest of the editor of the *Comic Times*, to which he had contributed some light verses. He suggested two anagrams of Charles Lutwidge – 'Edgar Cuthwellis' and 'Edgar U.C. Westhill' – but decided on 'Lewis Carroll', extracted, with typical Dodgsonian logic, from Lutwidge (a form of Ludovic or Louis) and from Charles (a form of Carolus). As we shall see, for Charles Dodgson, 'Lewis Carroll' was only a minor (if highly profitable) part of his life, and one that he was careful to keep separate from the rest of it as far as he could. He objected strongly when the Bodleian Library catalogue cross-referenced the mathematical works of Charles Dodgson with the more fantastic works of 'Lewis Carroll'. And so, as the 'Alice' books are made from the whole man, it seems most logical to stay with the name of the man, rather than the name of the mask.

PRELUDE

'Would you tell me, please, which way I ought to go from here?'

*Still, you know, words mean more than we mean to express when we use them:
so a whole book ought to mean a great deal more than the writer meant.*
– Charles Dodgson on *The Hunting of the Snark*[1]

In December 1865, the London publisher Macmillan brought out a book by a 33-year-old Oxford mathematics lecturer, Charles Dodgson. There had been some delay, because the quality of the first printing, which Dodgson had paid for himself – it had cost him nearly a year's salary – was not up to his meticulous standards. It was a children's book, but a rather curious one, for it was illustrated by the most famous satirical cartoonist of the day, John Tenniel, and even more curiously, it differed from almost every children's book that had come before it in that it didn't seem to have a moral. The book was *Alice's Adventures in Wonderland* and, 153 years later, it had become (with its sequel, *Through the Looking-Glass* (1872)) so much part of world culture that the Russian and British ambassadors to the United Nations, wrangling over the suspected poisoning of a spy in Britain, traded quotations from it.

The 'Alice' books are among the most quoted, most referenced, and most well-known (if not actually read) books in the English language, credited with changing the course of children's literature – of siding with the child readers to the point of anarchy. But that was not what has made them fascinating

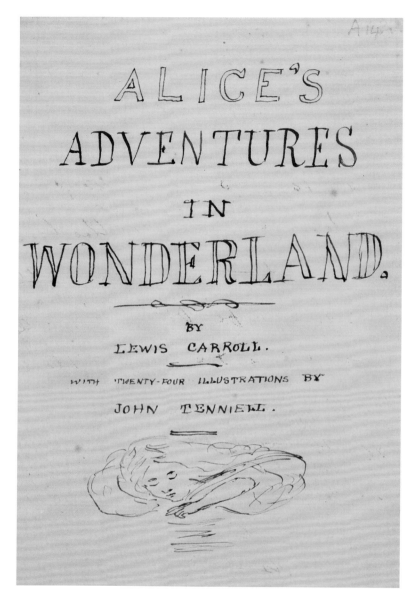

The meticulous Charles Dodgson took an interest in every part of the design of his books – even drafting the title page. This was probably the first attempt, some time in 1864: the illustration and the mis-spelling of Tenniel's name did not survive to the final version. The increase in the number of illustrations to the mystic number of 42 (see chapter 5) was still to come.

for the scholars and fans who have produced thousands of articles and hundreds of books about them. The books differ from most children's books that came before them (and most that have come after) in the sheer *density* of the writing: there is hardly a sentence that doesn't convey multiple meanings, multiple jokes, coded references to matters intellectual, political and personal. There are no longueurs, no padding, no lack of focus, hardly any deviation from a child-centred narrative voice: these are books in which an astonishingly versatile, complex and playful mind was communicating directly and empathetically with its audience. And Dodgson's mind was also profoundly that of a contradictory mid-Victorian – it is as well to remember that the writing of *Wonderland* and *Looking-Glass* almost exactly coincided with the midpoint of Queen Victoria's reign.

Trying to unravel the 'making of' the books is a particularly perilous task: so devious are the games that the author plays that anyone looking for the building blocks of the books is left with a texture of possibilities, probabilities, speculation and, very often, things so psychedelically ingenious that we wish them to be true. These books are a conspiracy theorist's dream!

Things are made even more challenging because there are *four* 'Alice' books: there is a manuscript version, *Alice's Adventures Under Ground*, which Dodgson gave to his child-friend Alice Liddell. He then developed this material into the published *Alice's Adventures in Wonderland*. Then, after five years of intermittent labour, came the sequel, *Through the Looking-Glass*. *Wonderland* and *Looking-Glass* have been so conflated in the minds of readers that even devotees (and certainly the British ambassador) find it hard to say which character appears in which book. Equally, while *Under Ground*, and, less so, *Wonderland* were written for *a* child, *Looking-Glass* was written for *children*, but, paradoxically, has an unmistakable personal and elegiac tone, remembering the lost child of the first book. And finally there is *The Nursery 'Alice'*, Dodgson's radical and sentimental (and to most modern readers, highly embarrassing) 1890 rewrite, aimed ostensibly at a younger market.

What Winston Churchill famously said about Russia in 1939 might well apply to the 'Alice' books: they are 'a riddle, wrapped in a mystery, inside an enigma; but perhaps there is a key.' This book looks for a key – although the task is as difficult as Alice's attempts to grasp the golden key in the great hall of *Wonderland*: we will have to do a great deal of shrinking, growing and splashing about.

Dodgson was, despite the image that we are often given of a reclusive lecturer living a quiet life among Oxford's dreaming spires, very much a man of his time. Not only was he keenly aware of social, cultural, and religious issues, but he was, like the Victorian period itself, a mass of contradictions. By his own account, the books were developed piecemeal: in writing out the first story, he noted, 'I added many fresh ideas, which seemed to grow of themselves upon the original stock.'

This book looks at the layers of ideas that went to make the 'Alice' books. First there is the world that the original Alice and her siblings would have recognized: *Under Ground* and *Wonderland* are full of private jokes and references. Then there is the world in which Dodgson lived: the world of Oxford, the world of politics big and small, the world of the Victorian religious and intellectual melee that swirled above the heads of the children. And then there is the private world inside Charles Dodgson's head. Humphrey Carpenter described Charles Kingsley, the man who wrote another (perhaps *the* other) famous children's book of the period, *The Water Babies*, as 'the first writer in England, perhaps the first in the world with the exception of Hans Andersen, to discover that a children's book can be the perfect vehicle for an adult's most personal and private concerns.'[2] Charles Dodgson would have agreed, but as a master of intellectual disguise, he was not, unlike Kingsley, inclined to wear his heart on his sleeve.

Charles Dodgson, lecturer in mathematics at Christ Church, aged twenty-six – an 'assisted self portrait', 2 June 1857. He wrote in his diary: 'Spent the morning at the Deanery ... The two dear little girls, Ina and Alice, were with me all the morning. To try the lens, I took a picture of myself, for which Ina took off the cap, and of course considered it all her doing.'

'My ideal child-friend.' An affectionate portrait of the enigmatic Alice Liddell, aged six, in the summer of 1858. Dodgson was using the 'wet collodion' photographic method, which produced glass-plate negatives (and considerable staining of the hands of the photographer).

Some words of warning, though, before we begin. Some critics agree with the first children's book historian, F.J. Harvey Darton, that '... there is not a back-hidden thought, an ulterior motive in the *Alices* from beginning to end.'[3] But most would agree with Derek Hudson's view that 'the "Alice" books were in some degree an autobiographical miscellany, woven together with extraordinary skill: an Odyssey of the subconscious.'[4]

Others are, like Martin Gardner, editor of *The Annotated Alice*, more cautious:

> The rub is that any work of nonsense abounds with so many inviting symbols that you can start with any assumption you please about the author and easily build up an impressive case for it ... The point here is ... that books of nonsense fantasy for children are not such fruitful sources of psychoanalytic insight as one might suppose them to be. They are much too rich in symbols. The symbols have too many explanations.[5]

Thus we will have to navigate between the poles of the too simple and literal, and the too complicated and speculative ... all of which brings us to a historic moment: a certain boat on a certain river on a particular day of a particular year.

1

TWO MEN AND THREE GIRLS IN A BOAT

Though she managed to pick plenty of beautiful rushes as the boat glided by, there was always a more lovely one that she couldn't reach.[1]

A lot of things amused the many-faceted Charles Dodgson, and one that surely would have done is the way in which the world has tried to turn his convoluted, obsessive and shape-shifting universe into a simple story.

Where better to start with this process than the most famous boat trip in fiction – or the most famous fictional boat trip. The day is Friday 4 July 1862. The scene is the River Thames near Oxford (known here, by a piece of Oxfordian whimsy, as the Isis). Two young clergymen, Charles Dodgson (twenty-nine) of Christ Church college (known as 'The House') rowing bow, and his friend Robinson Duckworth (twenty-seven), of Trinity College rowing stroke, are taking three of the daughters of the Dean of Christ Church – Lorina (thirteen), Alice (ten) and Edith (eight) – for a boat trip. There is nothing unusual about this: indeed, it is quite the fashion – and probably a politically shrewd one – for young lecturers to take the daughters of their senior colleagues for such outings. Possibly because the scenery on the way up the river to Osney is rather dull, the young ladies request a story – or the continuation of one – for this is not the first such expedition. Charles, who had as a teenager written stories for family magazines (including a satire on

'In the usual way,' Alice recalled in old age, 'after we had chosen our boat with great care, we three children were stowed away in the stern, and Mr Dodgson took the stroke oar.' John and Stephen Salter's boatyard, Folly Bridge, Oxford (c.1870), where the famous outing probably began.

Anglo-Saxon verse called 'Jabberwocky') and had contributed witty satirical verses to *Comic Times*, obliges.

Many years later – and it is as well to note that it *was* many years later – in 1899, Duckworth recalled the trip:

> … the story was actually composed and spoken *over my shoulder* for the benefit of Alice Liddell, who was acting as 'cox' of our gig. I remember turning round and saying, 'Dodgson, is this an extempore romance of yours?' And he replied, 'Yes I'm inventing as we go along.'[2]

Alice's father, the formidable Dean of Christ Church, Henry George Liddell (1811–1898) was no mean artist and had a talent for doodling. The sketches he produced with his gold pen on official pink blotting paper during college meetings between 1855 and 1891 became instant collectors' items.

(As it happened, Duckworth was not above helping with the tale, and apparently suggested the idea of the Mock Turtle.)

Alice Liddell herself, in her old age (she died in 1934), remembered – and we might use that word advisedly – 'that blazing summer afternoon', and Dodgson began the published version, *Alice's Adventures in Wonderland*, with a suitably idyllic verse:

> All in the golden afternoon
> Full leisurely we glide …
> Beneath such dreamy weather …

And of course, as we have seen, the story didn't stop there: when they got home, Dodgson wrote the story out as *Alice's Adventures Under Ground*, added his own illustrations, and gave it to Alice.

It makes a good story, and so it should, as most of it *is* a story: not that it was a deliberate fabrication, but Duckworth and the elderly Alice were only human in buying into the myth of the inception of what had in forty years become a bestseller and in seventy years had become an institution.

It is so charming a story that Oxford still celebrates Alice's Day each year – and has adopted 'Lewis Carroll' as one of its most famous sons – despite that fact that, thanks to the brevity of Oxford academic terms, he spent much (or most) of his time elsewhere. It is so charming, so appropriate for the birth of a children's book (there is a myth that the best ones – *Winnie-the-Pooh*, *Treasure Island*, *The Wind in the Willows*, *The Hobbit* – originated with stories for a specific child) that it doesn't really matter that, far from being a golden afternoon, the weather on that day was 'cool and rather wet'. Equally, it doesn't matter that *Wonderland* is almost certainly a confabulation of stories told on several river trips, several sunny and rainy picnics. In fact, Dodgson admitted this himself, twenty years or so later, when that river story had become a highly successful book, and the book a (slightly less successful) play. He pondered, in an article in *The Theatre* (April, 1887), upon how it came about:

> Many a day we had rowed together on that quiet stream – the three little maidens and I – and many a fairy tale had been extemporised for their benefit … yet none of these many tales got written down: they lived and died, like summer midges, each in its own golden afternoon until there came a day when, as it chanced, one of my little listeners petitioned that the tale might be written out for her.[3]

But what matters for a myth is that it *should have been* a single story told on a sunny day – and so, immortally, the myth has taken over reality.

Six months afterwards, on 10 February 1863, Dodgson, a meticulous, not to say obsessive, diarist, came back to his entry for 4 July and added the story

Alice's world: the door in the wall of the Deanery garden, open to Christ Church, Oxford's cathedral.

The Broad Walk, Christ Church, seen here in 1857, once included three elm trees planted by Alice and her sisters in 1863, while Charles Dodgson looked on, in honour of the wedding of the Prince and Princess of Wales.

of the telling of the story. Perhaps he shared Kenneth Grahame's view that second thoughts are 'always the best … and why should they not be truly ours, as much as the somewhat inadequate things that really come off?'[4] But, most of all, Dodgson, as good at marketing his stories as he was at most other things, knew how to milk the sentimental sensibilities of his fellow Victorians, and a tale told on a dreamy afternoon, in the heart of England with innocent auditors, was literally pure gold.

Dodgson claimed, perhaps disingenuously, that it was nothing to do with him:

Between 1868 and 1901, Thomas Shrimpton and Son, of Broad Street, Oxford, produced over 1000 photographic reproductions of caricatures, mostly by and for undergraduates. They often record incidents otherwise forgotten by history: here Dean Liddell flails unruly undergraduates outside the Sheldonian Theatre in c.1871.

Sometimes an idea came at night, when I had to get up and strike a light to write it down – sometimes when out on a lonely walk … but whenever or however it came, *it came of itself*. I cannot set invention going like a clock, by any voluntary winding-up: nor do I believe that any *original* writing (and what other writing is worth presenting?) was ever so produced … 'Alice' and the 'Looking-Glass' are made up almost wholly of bits and scraps, single ideas which came of themselves.[5]

But if the original story was not gifted by the river gods, where did it come from? Our search for the origins of some of these scraps may as well begin with that idyllic boat trip on the mythologized Isis.

of her own little sister. So the boat wound slowly along, beneath the bright summer-day, with its merry crew and its music of voices and laughter, till it passed round one of the many turnings of the stream, and she saw it no more.

Then she thought, (in a dream within the dream, as it were,) how this same little Alice would, in the after-time, be herself a grown woman: and how she would keep, through her riper years, the simple and loving heart of her childhood: and how she would gather around her other little children, and make their eyes bright and eager with many a wonderful tale, perhaps even with these very adventures of the little Alice of long-ago: and how she would feel with all their simple sorrows, and find a pleasure in all their simple joys, remembering her own child-life, and the happy summer-days. days.

Dodgson ended *Alice's Adventures Under Ground* with a cameo of Alice's face pasted into the manuscript. It had been cut from a copy of this photograph, taken in the Deanery garden in July 1860, when Alice was eight. It was not until 1977 that it was discovered that there was a hand-drawn portrait of Alice beneath it.

That boat was an outlier to a world of wealth and privilege: Christ Church, the Oxford college which also includes the city's cathedral, saw itself (and perhaps still does) as an elite college of the best university in the world. When they took the boat out, from Folly Bridge boatyard, both Duckworth and Dodgson were on the cusp of higher things: Duckworth was about to become tutor to Prince Leopold (youngest son of Queen Victoria) and

Dodgson was about to move into the best set of college rooms in Oxford, soon to be vacated by Lord Bute, overlooking Tom Quad and the archdeacon's garden in Christ Church (Stair 7 Room 3).

Their passengers were quite distinguished, too. They were the daughters of a well-connected and powerful figure, Dean Henry Liddell, and his forceful wife, Lorina. They figure in a somewhat a scurrilous student rhyme of the period, which nevertheless makes its point:

> I am the Dean, this Mrs Liddell.
> She plays first, I, second fiddle.
> She is the Broad,
> I am the High –
> We are the University

[Broad Street and High Street are the main streets of Oxford.]

The eldest daughter was Lorina Charlotte, known as Ina; the youngest, and thought by some – John Ruskin, for example – to be the prettiest, was Edith. And the one that concerns us most was Alice Pleasance, the fourth child and second daughter of ten children. And the first thing to say about the 'real' Alice is that in real life she looked nothing like almost any of the images of her in books or films.

Even though the 'Alice' books have been illustrated by well over a hundred artists, many readers rely for their mental images of the characters on the work of John Tenniel – Dodgson rarely describes them. And so it is easy to forget that the image of Alice in *Wonderland* and *Looking-Glass* is not Alice Liddell, but Tenniel's generalized idea of the fashionable Pre-Raphaelite type of girl (possibly one Mary Hilton Babcock, although Tenniel claimed not to use models). Even Dodgson's own illustrations in *Alice's Adventures Under Ground* portray Alice with long fair hair, rather than the short dark hair of the real girl.

ONE OF THE PLEASURES OF PHOTOGRAPHY. — VISITING COUNTRY HOUSES AND CALOTYPING ALL THE ELIGIBLE DAUGHTERS.

A sardonic illustration from Cuthbert Bede's *Photographic Pleasures* (1855). Dodgson, an outstanding amateur photographer, was more concerned with photographing celebrities, from Prince Leopold to the Rossettis, George MacDonald, Bishop Samuel Wilberforce and many more. Bede is best known for his witty portrait of Oxford undergraduate life – *The Adventures of Mr Verdant Green* (1853-7).

Nor do most images of Alice match the *age* of the character in the books: both *Under Ground* and *Wonderland* take place on Alice Liddell's seventh birthday – 4 May 1859. We know this because *Looking-Glass* is set exactly six months later, the day before Guy Fawkes night, 4 November. Alice watches from her window 'the boys getting in sticks for the bonfire ... Only it got so cold, and it snowed so, they had to leave off. Never mind, Kitty, we'll go and see the bonfire tomorrow.'[6] Alice confirms her age to Humpty Dumpty, which produces a characteristically mordant exchange:

'Seven years and six months!' Humpty Dumpty repeated thoughtfully. 'An uncomfortable sort of age. Now if you'd asked *my* advice, I'd have said "Leave off at seven" – but it's too late now.'

'I never ask advice about growing,' Alice said indignantly ... 'I mean ... one ca'n't help growing older.'

'*One* ca'n't, perhaps, said Humpty Dumpty; 'but *two* can. With proper assistance you might have left off at seven.'[7]

The closest that an actor has come to Alice's age in film and television adaptations has been Natalie Gregory in Harry Harris's 1985 television production (she was nine when it was filmed) and Kathryn Beaumont, who at the age of 10 voiced Alice in Disney's 1951 version. More characteristic have been Charlotte Henry in Norman McLeod's 1933 star-packed Paramount film (nineteen), Fiona Fullerton in William Sterling' 1972 version (fifteen) and Anne-Marie Mallik (thirteen) in Jonathan Miller's controversial 1966 television adaptation. Most recently, Mia Wasikowska played Alice in Tim Burton's *Alice in Wonderland* (2010) at twenty-one, and in the sequel *Alice Through the Looking-Glass* (James Bobin, 2016) at twenty-seven. Only in Dennis Potter's *Dreamchild* (Gavin Millar, 1985) does the actor (Amelia Shankley (twelve)) resemble Alice Liddell. These are not, however, necessarily misrepresentations for although the books were in one degree or another written for the 'real' Alice, Alice Liddell was not the only 'child-friend' in Dodgson's life – nor the only one called Alice. As with almost everything about these books, we are looking at something with many layers.

The man rowing bow is no more easily accessible. Charles Dodgson, son of a Cheshire Vicar (an ex Christ Church man) had been at the House for eleven years: he was a mathematician, and not a particularly good teacher – at least, he was not good at dealing with unruly undergraduates. He had recently taken deacon's orders to fulfil the residentiary requirements of Christ Church, but rarely preached. Which perhaps makes him sound rather dull, and the fact that he produced the 'Alice' books all the more remarkable.

'A good old-fashioned Rectory, with no *beauty* outside or inside.' So wrote Dodgson's father, describing the family home at Croft-on-Tees from 1843 to 1868. Here, the young Charles wrote family magazines for the entertainment of his seven sisters and three brothers.

But, as with most things about Dodgson, appearances could be deceptive. He was a very busy man. A pioneering photographer, he had bought his first camera in 1856 and by 1862 had taken pictures not only of Oxford friends but of the Poet Laureate, Alfred, Lord Tennyson; by 1865 he had added the illustrator Arthur Hughes, the writer George MacDonald and his children, the artist John Everett Millais and his wife, Effie (who we shall meet again), the Rossettis, Tom Taylor, the editor of *Punch*, and the actor Ellen Terry to his portfolio. Dodgson was also an avid theatre-goer (despite the high Anglican church frowning upon such things) and spent a lot of time in London, to the extent that he stayed regularly at specific hotels – in the 1860s first at

Another photograph from the Deanery garden in June 1857. In that year, Dodgson photographed his first great celebrities, the Tennyson family, and published a comic poem, 'Hiawatha's Photographing', in the magazine *The Train*.

Bridge across the River Thames at Godstow, near Oxford, 1835. Painting by Edward William Cooke (1811–1880).

Old Hummums Hotel in Covent Garden, and in 1865 at the Trafalgar Hotel in Spring Gardens.

Nor was Oxford his only centre of activities. He was the eldest boy and third child of eleven children, and remained close to his siblings (especially after his father died in 1868) – two of his brothers were also at Oxford. The long vacations were spent with his sisters at Croft-on-Tees (later at Guildford), and with his cousins in Sunderland, and he took regular rooms for many weeks of his summers at Whitby (and later at Eastbourne).

However, when he *was* at Christ Church, he was at one of the country's major centres of cultural debates (as well as petty squabbles) – notably the battles over Charles Darwin's theories of evolution, and the high and broad factions of the Church of England. As an expert on logic, but with a conventionally pious background and an ingenious mind and imagination, Dodgson was not the man to ignore the disputes, large and small, going on around him. Like any individualist he could be an awkward customer, and by 1862 had already begun feuds that lasted a lifetime.

He was also something of an obsessive – he had begun his diary in 1853 (it eventually ran to thirteen volumes) and his 'Register of Letters Sent and Received' in 1861 (it eventually recorded 98,721 items) – and at his epistolary peak he wrote more than 2,000 letters a year. He had traits of perfectionism that were going to plague his illustrators and his publishers, as well as his colleagues at Christ Church. He had also begun to build up his personal library, which eventually extended to about 4,200 volumes representing about 2,500 titles.[8] They show an astonishing range of interests – although perhaps only characteristic of an educated Victorian: there is science (both pro-Darwin and anti-Darwin), homeopathy, magic, astrology, the Koran, books on Buddhism, women's rights, prostitution, art, linguistics, theatre, the circus and politics (notably the 'Irish Question'). And he had already published *The Fifth Book of Euclid Treated Algebraically* (1858) and *A Syllabus of Plane Algebraic Geometry* (1860).

But in 1862, on the river, in that mythical moment, he was just a slightly eccentric, amusing young man, happy to entertain a boatload of admiring girls with stories that 'came of themselves'. And yet stories and books – and perhaps especially children's books – do not exist in an idyllic bubble: the forces of genre and the memories of a lifetime of reading conspire together, and so it is not surprising that the tale told over Duckworth's shoulder turns out to be not quite the evanescent mayfly that Dodgson claimed.

2

BEFORE ALICE

I distinctly remember ... how, in a desperate attempt to strike out some new line of fairy-lore, I ... sent my heroine straight down a rabbit-hole ... without the least idea what was to happen afterwards.
– Charles Dodgson, 1887[1]

The 'Alice' stories have a high reputation for changing the face of children's books – *Wonderland* 'revolutionised children's literature';[2] it was 'the first ... unapologetic appearance in print, for readers who sorely needed it, of liberty of thought'.[3] Whether this is actually true has been in doubt for a long time: one of the earliest critics of children's books, Edward Salmon, noted in 1887 that although *Wonderland* and *Looking-Glass* 'are, of course, undeniably clever and possess many charms exclusively their own, there is nothing extraordinarily original about either ...'[4] The truth may lie in the making of the books.

The first commercial English children's books date from the 1740s and were advertised as being 'for instruction and delight', and by the time Charles Dodgson came to write his, the emphasis was still on instruction (moral and religious). He was certainly well acquainted with the literary furniture of childhood; as a well-read child, and an adult with five younger sisters – the youngest, Henrietta, eleven years younger – and a man with considerable empathy for children, he knew how they felt about the books they were given.

Some of the earliest books aimed at children were collections of hymns, notably Isaac Watts's *Divine Songs Attempted in Easy Language for the Use of Children* (1715): Dodgson was never one to resist a lampoon, so the poor fictional Alice, as much a reciter as her live counterpart, finds herself struggling with Watts's 'The Sluggard':

'Tis the Voice of the Sluggard. I hear him complain
You have wak'd me too soon, I must slumber again

which emerges as

'Tis the voice of the Lobster: I heard him declare
'You have baked me too brown, I must sugar my hair.'[5]

As the Gryphon remarks, 'That's different from what *I* used to say when I was a child.' Quite so.

Watts's 'Against Idleness and Mischief' gets the same treatment.

How doth the little busy bee
   Improve each shining hour,
And gather honey all the day
   From ev'ry op'ning flower!

How skilfully she builds her cell!
   How neat she spreads the wax!
And labours hard to store it well
   With the sweet food she makes.

By 1902, Alice's encounter with the Gryphon and the Mock Turtle had found its way into a series of hugely popular magic lantern slides – the 'Junior Lecturers Series' published by W. Butcher and Sons of Blackheath. The *Alice in Wonderland* set, copied more or less accurately from Tenniel's drawings, covered the first three chapters of the book in twenty-four slides. This is number 19.

Alice underground can manage only:

How doth the little crocodile
  Improve his shining tail,
And pour the waters of the Nile
  On every golden scale!

How cheerfully he seems to grin,
  And neatly spreads his claws!
And welcomes little fishes in,
  With gently smiling jaws![6]

Some of Watts's imitators were in Dodgson's library, notably *Hymns in Prose for Children* (1781 – Dodgson's copy was printed in 1845) by the redoubtable Anna Laetitia Barbauld, purveyor of educational material to the young. As Charles Lamb wrote in exasperation to his friend Samuel Taylor Coleridge in 1802:

Mrs Barbauld's stuff has banished all the old classics of the nursery … Think what you would have been now, if instead of being fed with tales and old wives' fables in childhood, you had been crammed with geography and history.[7]

Dodgson owned (and had obviously read) many of the key books produced by the utilitarianists and evangelicals – tractarians who had dominated late eighteenth-century children's writing, and whose influence lingered through much of the nineteenth. Among them were Sarah Trimmer's *Fabulous Histories* (1786) with its moralistic talking birds, Hannah More's self-explanatory *Cheap Repository Tracts* (from 1795), and Maria Edgeworth's *Early Lessons* (1801). The most famous of these lessons is probably 'The Purple Jar', which first appeared in *The Parent's Assistant* (1796), in which Rosamond chooses a pretty jar over a pair of shoes, and then finds that it is a plain jar filled with purple liquid. As a result, her father refuses to take her on an excursion because of the state of her shoes. While such raw moralizing has given these writers a rather severe reputation, the children they portray are very often lively and 'natural' – closer to Alice than we might think.

But the moral hand was firm. Some of the favourite weapons of such writers were the 'awful warnings' epitomized by the 'tough love' approach of the parents in Mary Martha Sherwood's major bestseller *The Fairchild Family* (1818 and sequels), in which the children are taken on a visit to a gibbet to encourage them not to quarrel. In verse, a characteristic example is Elizabeth Turner's *The Daisy, or Cautionary Stories in Verse Adapted to the Ideas of Children from Four to Eight Years Old* (1807):

Poor Peter was burnt by the poker one day,
　　When he made it look pretty and red!
For the beautiful sparks made him think it fine play,
　　To lift it as high as his head …

Now if Peter had minded his Mother's command,
　　His fingers would not have been sore;
And he promised again, as she bound up his hand,
　　To play with hot pokers no more.

Dodgson seems to have been a satirist almost from the egg. In 1845, aged thirteen, he wrote a satirical verse, 'My Fairy'. His fairy forbids him to do virtually anything:

If, full of mirth, I smile and grin,
　　It says 'You must not laugh';
When once I wished to drink some gin
　　It said, 'You must not quaff'.

Moral: 'You mustn't.'[8]

And when he came to write the 'Alice' books, he was clearly sympathetic to the sufferings of young readers who had endured such books at length. When Alice encounters a bottle labelled 'Drink Me', the narrator comments:

> It was all very well to say 'Drink Me,' but the wise little Alice was not going to do *that* in a hurry. 'No, I'll look first,' she said, 'and see whether it's marked *"poison"* or not'; for she had read several nice little stories about children who had got burnt, and eaten up by wild beasts, and other unpleasant things, all because they *would* not remember the simple rules their friends had taught them: such as, that a red-hot poker will burn you if you hold it too long; and that, if you cut your finger *very* deeply with a knife, it usually bleeds; and she had never forgotten that, if you drink much from a bottle marked 'poison', it is almost certain to disagree with you, sooner or later.[9]

As the Duchess observed, in *Wonderland*:

> 'You're thinking about something, my dear, and that makes you forget to talk. I ca'n't tell you just now what the moral of that is, but I shall remember it in a bit.'
> 'Perhaps it hasn't one,' Alice ventured to remark.
> Tut, tut, child!' said the Duchess. 'Everything's got a moral, if only you can find it.'[10]

His (fairly) good-natured garbling of respectable texts was also applied to Mary Howitt's famous 'The Spider and the Fly', from *The New Year's Gift* (1829), a poem in the 'awful warning' tradition. (Howitt was one of the first translators of Hans Christian Andersen's stories into English.)

> 'Will you walk into my parlour?' said the Spider to the Fly,
> ''Tis the prettiest little parlour that ever you did spy ...'

... becomes in the hands, or flippers, of the Mock Turtle:

'Will you walk a little faster?' said a whiting to a snail,
'There's a porpoise close behind us, and he's treading on my tail ...'[11]

Of course, Dodgson wasn't the first to send up this literature. There is the story (another literary legend) of the Frankfurt paediatrician Heinrich Hoffmann (1809–1894), who, unable to find anything for his children's Christmas presents in 1844 except 'awful warning' tales, produced a parody in 1845 which found its (bestselling) way into English as *The English Struwwelpeter; or, Pretty Stories and Funny Pictures for Little Children* (1848). These included the 'great, long, red-legged scissorman' who cuts off the thumbs of thumb-suckers, and 'The Dreadful Story of Pauline and the Matches', when Minz and Maunz, the pussy-cats, sit by Pauline's ashes and produce a pool of tears.

Their tears ran down their cheeks so fast,
They made a little pool at last.

As the century had gone by, other cracks in the humourless approach to children's books appeared (a humourless approach all the more odd in that the Victorians, to judge from their periodicals, had an insatiable appetite for riddles and puns and nonsense). The most famous example of 'liberalization' is probably Catherine Sinclair's *Holiday House* (1839). At first sight this is in the tradition of *The Fairchild Family*, complete with lachrymose deathbed scene, but the naughty children – in one episode, Laura cuts off her own hair and Harry sets fire to the nursery – are drawn sympathetically, and are surrounded by ironic adults. As the narrator observes:

Harry and Laura became, from this time, two of the most heedless, frolicsome beings in the world, and had to be whipped almost every morning; for in those days it had not been discovered that children can be made good without it ...

'Shockheaded Peter' – the trailblazing, iconoclastic and nightmarish parody of the 'awful warning' genre of children's books – here in an edition from the 1890s.

Dodgson gave the Liddell girls a copy of *Holiday House* in 1861, with an acrostic poem – each line beginning with the letters of their names, Lorina, Alice and Edith:

> Little maidens, when you look
> On this little story-book,
> Reading with attentive eye
> Its enticing history,
> Never think that hours of play
> Are your only HOLIDAY.
> And that in a HOUSE of joy
> Lessons serve but to annoy …[12]

He also gave Lorina a copy of Elizabeth Wetherell's *Mr Rutherford's Children* (1853), another story of lively children, light on moral teaching.

Dodgson, then, was steeped in childhood culture of all kinds. He also owned *Parables from Nature* (first series 1855) by the prolific Margaret Gatty (who founded the influential *Aunt Judy's Magazine* in 1866) in which there is a story, 'Training and Restraining', about the conversation of flowers. The wicked wind first persuades them that being tied to sticks is a bad thing, and then blows them all down. The daughter of the family, grieving over the mess, says to her mother

> 'I quite understand what you have so often said about the necessity of training, and restraint, and culture, for us as well as for flowers, in a fallen world.'

And so when Alice, down the rabbit hole, sees 'the loveliest garden you ever saw [with] beds of bright flowers and … cool fountains', she was part of a literary–cultural fashion.[13] Gardens were a common Pre-Raphaelite motif, and the involvement of children in gardening, with books such as the Revd

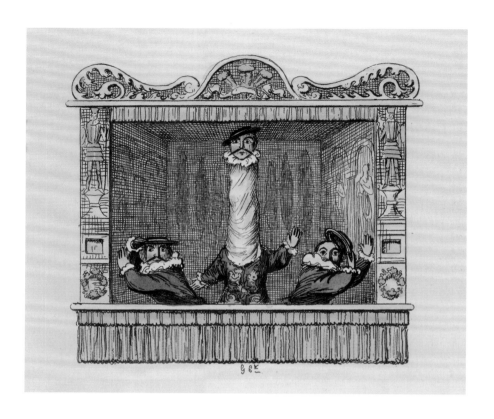

C.A. Johns's *Gardening for Children* (*c*.1848) was soon to blossom, as it were, into a national craze. The idea of the small door into the lovely garden echoes down to Frances Hodgson Burnett's *The Secret Garden* (1911) and far beyond.

Perhaps more obviously, nursery rhymes pepper the 'Alice' books: the Queen of Hearts and her tarts, Humpty Dumpty, Tweedledum and Tweedledee, and the Lion and Unicorn provide major episodes; traditional songs such as 'Here We Go Round the Mulberry Bush' casually appear, and an old lullaby is gently parodied:

> *Hush-a-by lady, in Alice's lap*
> *Till the feast's ready we've time for a nap:*[14]

The image of Alice's long neck has been traced to various Freudian symbols, to the fire-irons in the Deanery, and perhaps most plausibly to George Cruickshank's illustration of *Punch and Judy*, first published in 1828.

There are traces of parlour games ('animal, vegetable or mineral?'); fables, which were becoming fashionable (Tenniel had illustrated an edition of *Aesop* in 1848), in tags such as 'down, down, down'; and even of pantomime.[15] Although Dodgson did not see his first pantomime until 17 January 1866 (*Little King Pippin*, produced by Percy Roselle at Drury Lane) their elements cannot have passed him by, with their slapstick kitchen scenes, and characters as playing cards. His diaries record more than 300 visits to the theatre and he would have seen the trial scenes in Dion Boucicault's *Janet Pride* (1856, 1864) and *The Trial of Effie Deans* (1863). Some of the inspiration for *Looking-Glass* may have come from *Harlequin King Chess* (1865–6), and one of the standard pantomimes of the day was *Pat a Cake*, which features a magic chessboard.[16]

In John Payne Collier's *The Tragical Comedy or Comical Tragedy of Punch and Judy* (1832) there is even an illustration by George Cruickshank to this scene:

> ACT II
>
> Enter a FIGURE dressed like a courtier. He ... stops in the centre; the music ceases, and suddenly his throat begins to elongate, and his head gradually rises until his neck is taller than all the rest of his body. After pausing for some time, the head sinks again; and, as soon as it has descended to its natural place, the FIGURE *exit*.[17]

The influence of other children's books is more difficult to detect, but Dodgson also owned Crowquill's *Comic Nursery Tales* series from the 1840s, William Brighty Rands' *Lilliput Levee* (1864), and Felix Summerley's *Home Treasury* (1846). It is perhaps surprising that Dodgson does not seem to have been influenced by Edward Lear's *A Book of Nonsense* (1846, 1861) – he and Lear never met nor ever refer to each other in their letters and journals – and the limerick form is conspicuously absent from the 'Alice' books. However, there is a similarity between Lear's illustrations for his nonsense books, and Dodgson's for *Under Ground.*

There *were* two books that directly influenced Dodgson, although in different ways. He had been a friend of George MacDonald and his family since 1859, and greatly admired MacDonald's first venture into fantasy, *Phantastes* (1858). This pioneering fantasy has few, if any, direct resemblances to the 'Alice' books, but despite the Spenserian allegorical air (which MacDonald denied), it has a freewheeling inventiveness in a different world that clearly appealed to Dodgson.

More contentious is the relationship of the 'Alice' books to Charles Kingsley's *The Water Babies*, first published in *Macmillan's Magazine* (August 1862 to March 1863). It could well be that Dodgson reacted to the flamboyant Kingsley's overt didacticism in what purported to be a children's book. Kingsley was happy to use the children's book for 'educational' purposes, thus betraying the contract with the child reader. *The Water Babies* abounds in energetic interpolations – rants – on a huge range of topics: for example, when Pandora's box is opened, out come, flying over his child readers' heads, Kingsley's assorted prejudices:

> Measles, Famines, Monks, Quacks, Scarlatina, Unpaid bills, Idols, Tight stays, Hooping-coughs, Potatoes, Popes, Bad Wine, Wars, Despots, Peace-mongers, Demagogues, And, worst of all, Naughty Boys and Girls.[18]

Dodgson did not meddle with some genres – the school story, or the sea story, or even the 'waif' novels, such as Maria Louisa Charlesworth's bestselling *Ministering Children* (1854) – but when it came to fantasy he would not see it so manipulated. Even worse was Kingsley's jovial but patronizing mode of address. *The Water Babies* begins:

> Once upon a time there was a little chimney-sweep, and his name was Tom. That is a short name, and you have heard it before, so you will not have much trouble in remembering it.

But if Dodgson was remarkable for maintaining an honest contract with his readers, he could not avoid bringing to the books the Victorian weakness for the romantic chivalric legacy of Scott, and for maudlin sentimentality. In 1874 he gave Alice Liddell a copy of Florence Montgomery's *Misunderstood* (1872) – very much a standard adult 'weepie', with a child accident and a deathbed scene. Equally, as we shall see, he had a wide knowledge of the

The highlight of the pantomime *Harlequin King Chess or Tom the Piper's Son and See-Saw Marjery Daw* at the Surrey Theatre in 1865 was a game of chess with live players in the final act. The *Illustrated London News* (30 December) featured the image '"King Chess" – giving check to the queen'. The opening night was so popular that Blackfriars Road, leading to the theatre, was blocked by crowds.

more heart-rending drawing-room ballads. The trial of the Knave of Hearts is a parody of the sensation novels, literally millions of copies of which were devoured by the masses, while the White Queen, by Dodgson's own admission, was derived from a character in one of the more respectable of these, Mrs Wragge in Wilkie Collins' *No Name.* Mrs Wragge is 'notably feeble-minded' – and the White Queen is transmogrified into a sheep.

Dodgson could kick some of the fashions quite hard when he had a mind to. He had known and photographed the Tennysons since 1857, but by the time of *Looking-Glass* they had fallen out, and Dodgson felt he was the injured party. He took his revenge on one of Tennyson's most famous poems, 'Maud', in which a lover is waiting in a flower garden. It begins

Come into the garden, Maud
  For the black bat, night, has flown …

The poet then talks to the lily, rose, and passion-flower, who all listen for Maud:

There has fallen a splendid tear
  From the passion-flower at the gate.
She is coming, my dove, my dear;
  She is coming, my life, my fate;

The red rose cries, 'She is near, she is near;'
  And the white rose weeps, 'She is late;'
The larkspur listens, 'I hear, I hear;'
  And the lily whispers, 'I wait.'

She is coming, my own, my sweet;
  Were it ever so airy a tread …

In Dodgson's irreverent version, Alice and the flowers are listening for the Red Queen:

'She's coming!' cried the Larkspur: 'I hear her footstep, thump, thump, along the gravel walk.'

Alice's major floral interlocutor is the Tiger-lily: in the original manuscript of *Looking-Glass* Dodgson had followed Tennyson by including the passion-flower, until someone pointed out to him that the passion referred to was the passion of Christ. Dodgson, who, like his father, was sensitive to such matters, changed it.

Compared to Wordsworth, Tennyson got off lightly. In October 1856 Dodgson had published a parody of Wordsworth's 'Resolution and

Sweeping sleeping symbolism? Tom the soot-grimed chimney-sweep finds himself in the pure bedroom of little Ellie in Charles Kingsley's *The Water Babies* (1863): this was the kind of literary strategy of which Dodgson deeply disapproved. An illustration by the American Jessie Willcox Smith from a 1916 edition.

Independence', called 'Upon the Lonely Moor', in the humorous magazine *The Train*. The version in *Looking-Glass* reaches virtuoso heights of sarcasm. Wordsworth's narrator meets an old leech-gatherer, and asks him what he does for a living: the old man tells him, but the poet's mind wanders …

And now, not knowing what the Old Man had said,
My question eagerly did I renew,
'How is it that you live, and what is it you do?'
He with a smile did then his words repeat …

Needless to say, in Dodgson's version, things become a little exaggerated:

'Who are you, aged man?' I said.
  'And how is it you live?'
His answer trickled through my head,
  Like water through a sieve …

So, having no reply to give
  To what the old man said,
I cried 'Come tell me how you live!'
  And thumped him on the head …[19]

But perhaps the most telling example of the multiple sources of 'Alice', and the way in which Dodgson absorbed and adapted them, is the case of J.J. Grandville (1803–1847).

Grandville was a French satirical artist, famous for adding animal heads to human figures in his drawings, and he worked for the Parisian magazine *Le Charivari*. The great British satirical equivalent magazine, *Punch*, was subtitled for some years *The London Charivari*, and one of its major contributors was John Tenniel, Dodgson's carefully chosen, and much put-upon, illustrator. Tenniel was much influenced by Grandville, and it has often been pointed out that the illustration of the Frog Footman in *Wonderland* and the Frog Gardener in *Looking-Glass* are very much in Grandville's style. But that is not all: Grandville also produced a collection – *Les fleurs animées* [*The Flowers Personified*] (1847) – of which the 'Garden of Live flowers' in *Looking-Glass* is very reminiscent.

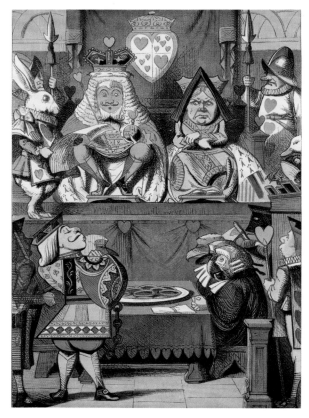

The hidden source? Both the spirit and the images of J.J. Grandville permeate Tenniel's illustrations (above) and Dodgson's text: 'La bataille des cartes' (opposite) is just one of many episodes which bear a resemblance to *Alice's Adventures in Wonderland*.

Yet even more striking is a comparison of the illustration of the royal garden party with 'La bataille des cartes' from Grandville's *Un Autre Monde* (1844), and there are many other echoes.

And so, apart from floating on the Isis, the ideas for the Alice books were already floating on a century of children's literature and popular culture and art: what was needed now was for Dodgson to add those personal details that would appeal to the real Alice and her sisters.

LA BATAILLE DES CARTES.

3

WHAT ALICE KNEW

When I used to read fairy tales, I fancied that sort of thing never happened, and now here I am in the middle of one! There ought to be a book written about me, that there ought![1]

To judge from the perennially healthy sales of 'personalized' children's books, Alice Liddell, at the age of twelve, might have been delighted to have received *Alice's Adventures Under Ground* – a handwritten and illustrated book which featured herself as central character. What the rest of her siblings thought about this is not recorded, nor is how she and her family responded to the fame, or notoriety, that the publication of *Alice's Adventures in Wonderland* brought. Equally, what a nineteen-year-old Alice though of *another* book, *Looking-Glass*, featuring her seven-year-old self, and ending with an explicit acrostic love poem to her, might give one pause.

But, at least initially, the in-jokes and references in *Under Ground*, even when diluted or modified in *Wonderland* and *Looking-Glass*, must have been great fun. Dodgson was more than ably abetted by Tenniel – the image of the dome of the Water Lily House in the Oxford Botanic Garden behind the Queen's Croquet-Ground, or the eel traps (at Godstow north-west of Oxford) behind the eel-balancing Father William, or the Sheep's shop at St Aldate's, almost across the road from Christ Church, are all real places that the real Alice would have recognized.

Alice Liddell lived in the Deanery at Christ Church, and Queen Alice's doorway is the doorway of the Chapter House. There is also (again thanks to Tenniel) a resemblance between the fire irons in the Deanery and Alice with her long neck in *Wonderland*. The Liddell sisters would have played croquet, and indeed had recently been playing it with the Revd Dodgson, and he had invented a game called 'Castle Croquet' (privately printed version 1863). He frequently played cards with them – not surprisingly, he invented a game called 'Court Circular' – and taught them to play chess.

It is all very personal. Dodgson was not above describing directly (or so we can assume), the Alice he knew:

> She generally gave herself very good advice … and sometimes she scolded herself so severely as to bring tears into her eyes; and once she remembered trying to box her own ears for having cheated herself in a game of croquet she was playing against herself, for this curious child was very fond of pretending to be two people.[2]

Then there is a reference to Alice's trip to Llandudno in 1861 (her father had a house built there in 1865):

> Alice had been to the seaside once in her life, and had come to the general conclusion that, wherever you go on the English coast, you find a number of bathing machines in the sea, some children digging in the sand with wooden spades, then a row of lodging-houses, and behind them a railway-station.[3]

Again, in *Looking-Glass*, the characterization seems to be drawn from life – 'here came the favourite little toss of the head' – and there is what sounds like an authentic story:

Local architecture: the dome of Oxford's Water Lily House, built in 1851 to grow the giant Amazonian water lily, appears at the back of the Red Queen's croquet lawn. (The White Queen's favourite little pawn in *Looking-Glass* is, of course, called Lily.) The keeper of the gardens in Dodgson's time was Professor Charles Daubeny, a supporter of Darwin.

The Queen has come!   And *isn't* she angry?
Oh, my poor little Alice!

And here I wish I could tell you half the things Alice used to say, beginning with her favourite phrase 'Let's pretend.' She had had quite a long argument with her sister only the day before – all because Alice had begun with 'Let's pretend we're kings and queens;' and her sister, who liked being very exact, had argued that they couldn't because there were only two of them, and Alice had been reduced at last to say 'Well, you can be one of them, then, and *I'll* be all the rest.[4]

From the beginning of *Under Ground* the jokes are very local. The White Rabbit might well have been a portrait of Dr Henry Wentworth, Professor of Medicine and the Liddells' doctor. As Alice falls down the rabbit-hole, she 'took down a jar from one of the shelves as she passed: it was labelled ORANGE MARMALADE.'[5] A small thing, perhaps, but not if you knew, as Alice would have done, that her mother had a particularly good marmalade recipe. It was so good that she gave it to a Mrs Frank Cooper of Oxford – and it is still produced 'for discerning palates'. (As the eponymous Missee Lee, the Cambridge-educated pirate, says in Arthur Ransome's novel: 'Better scholars, better plofessors at Camblidge, but better marmalade at Oxford.')[6]

Also, on her way down, Alice reflects, in one of the first death jokes in the books: '"Why, I wouldn't say anything about it, even if I fell off the top of the house!" (Which was most likely true.)' And of course, to a Christ Church girl, there was really only one 'house'.

Up to this point, *Under Ground* and *Wonderland* are very similar, but Dodgson began to make changes for the published version. In *Under Ground*, Alice wonders whether she might have been changed into Gertrude ('I'm sure I'm not Gertrude … for her hair goes in such long ringlets') or Florence ('I'm sure I ca'n't be Florence, for I know all sorts of things, and she, oh! she

A very Edwardian Alice, this illustration for the Bodley Head edition of *Alice's Adventures in Wonderland* (1907) is by W.H. Walker (1854–1940), who as William Henry Romaine-Walker designed parts of the Tate Gallery and the British Museum.

An unused sketch by Dodgson for *Alice's Adventures Under Ground* (1863–4); only the mouse survived into the final versions.

knows such a very little ... I must be Florence after all, and I shall have to go and live in that poky little house, and have next to no toys to play with, and oh! ever so many lessons to learn!').[7] Gertrude and Florence were cousins of the Liddells and so it is perhaps not surprising that Dodgson changed the names to Ada and Mabel for public consumption (the real Alice being something of a snob).

Arthur Rackham's meticulous, and perhaps unsettling, vision of the cast of the Caucus Race, from his 1907 edition. Rackham was a leading figure in the golden age of British book illustration, and his pictures for 'Alice', together with those of Tenniel, were a major inspiration for the Ruralist movement of artists of the late twentieth century.

The pool of tears is also full of familiar faces: 'There was a Duck and a Dodo, a Lory and an Eaglet, and several other curious creatures.'[8] The Duck was obviously Duckworth, and the Dodo the stammering Dodgson ('Do-do-dodgson'). When the facsimile of *Under Ground* came out in 1886, Dodgson inscribed Duckworth's copy: 'The Duck from the Dodo'. The Eaglet must be Alice's younger sister, Edith, and the Lory her elder sister, Lorina. 'Indeed, she had quite a long argument with the Lory, who at last turned sulky, and would only say "I am older than you, and must know better."' (A lory, happily, is a small parrot.) In *Under Ground*, Dodgson rather rubs in the sisterly joke, as Alice reflects:

> I do wish some of them had stayed a little longer! I was becoming such friends with them – really, the Lory and I were almost like sisters! And so was that dear little Eaglet![9]

Dinah, whose name is so powerful, was a real Dinah, a tabby owned by the Liddell children, and mother of the kittens in *Looking-Glass*. (Dinah was named – curiously enough – after the rich and suicidal daughter in a popular song 'Vilikins and his Dinah' (1854).)

The aftermath of the pool of tears episode is the most striking example of Dodgson at first borrowing directly from Alice's life, and then modifying the account for public consumption.

Dodgson's diary entry for Tuesday 17 June 1862 recounts a boat trip to Nuneham with his two elder sisters, Frances and Elizabeth, his aunt, Lucy Lutwidge, the Liddell girls, and Duckworth. It rained heavily, so they disembarked, and Dodgson walked on ahead with the children

> to the only house I knew in Sandford, Mrs Boughton's … I left them with her to get their clothes dried, and went off to find a vehicle, but none was to be had there, so on the others arriving, Duckworth and I walked on to Iffley, whence we sent them a fly [a hired coach].[10]

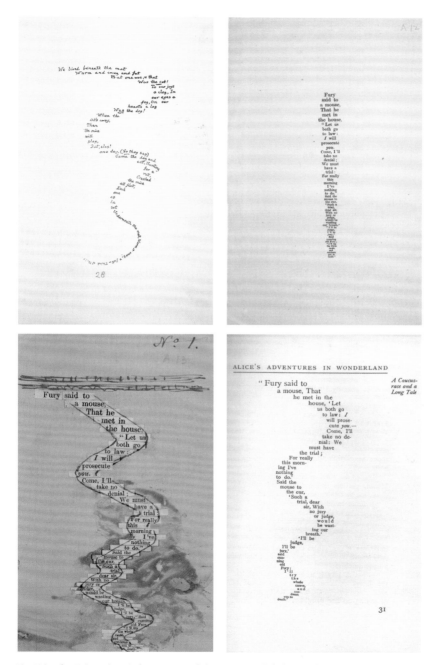

The Tale of a Tail: Dodgson's first version of the Mouse's tale/tail, in *Under Ground*, was rewritten in rather more dramatic style for *Wonderland*. He then had the printer print off the text in a single column, which he cut up and stuck together for the printer to reset.

In *Under Ground*, this is sketched almost to the life:

'I only meant to say,' said the Dodo in a rather offended tone, 'that I know of a house near here, where we could get the young lady and the rest of the party dried, and then we could listen comfortably to the story which I think you were good enough to promise to tell us,' bowing gravely to the mouse.

The mouse made no objection to this, and the whole party moved along the river bank, (for the pool had by this time begun to flow out of the hall, and the edge of it was fringed with rushes and forget-me-nots,) in a slow procession, the Dodo leading the way. After a time the Dodo became impatient, and, leaving the Duck to bring up the rest of the party, moved on at a quicker pace with Alice, the Lory, and the Eaglet, and soon brought them to a little cottage, and there they sat snugly by the fire, wrapped up in blankets, until the rest of the party had arrived, and they were all dry again.[11]

But this circumstantiality may have seemed rather dull for general consumption, so in *Wonderland* it was replaced by the caucus race, the Mouse's long tale, and the driest thing that the Mouse knows. This is the tale of Edwin and Morcar, an extract from Havilland Chepmell's *A Short Course of History* (1849) which the Liddells' governess, Miss Prickett ('Pricks'), was using with the children. This has led some investigators to suggest that the Mouse might be a satire on that good lady (she has also been identified as the 'spiky' Red Queen) – however, as we shall see, she seems to have been too formidable to be the Mouse and too kind to have been the Queen.

The Liddell sisters appear again in *Wonderland* at the Hatter's mad tea-party – one of those episodes so rich in personal reference that it needs a paragraph or two to itself. We will look at the identity of the Hatter and the Dormouse (no one seems bothered about the identity of the Hare) when we delve into Dodgson's world, but for now, the Dormouse is telling his story, and it could hardly be *more* about the Liddells.

Alice, Lorina and Harry, their eldest brother, all married comfortably, although perhaps not as well as their mother (who Dodgson once referred to as 'the Kingfisher') might have wished. Edith died suddenly of peritonitis in 1876 at the age of twenty-two, thirteen days after having become engaged.

'Once upon a time there were three little sisters,' the Dormouse began in a great hurry; 'and their names were Elsie, Lacie, and Tillie; and they lived at the bottom of a well –'

'What did they live on?' said Alice, who always took a great interest in questions of eating and drinking.

'They lived on treacle,' said the Dormouse, after thinking a minute or two …
'It was a treacle-well.'

'There's no such thing!'[12]

A rather less-than-elegant version of the 'three little sisters' who lived in a treacle well – with their treacle buckets: illustration by W.H. Walker (c.1907).

The three Liddell sisters are thinly disguised: Lorina Charlotte's initials were L.C.; Lacie is an anagram of Alice; and Tillie is short for Matilda, which was Edith's nickname. And the treacle well was, and is, not nonsense: treacle wells were healing wells or springs (treacle was another word for 'balm' – a soothing ointment – as in the 'treacle bibles' of 1568, which read, at Jeremiah 8: 22, 'Is there not treacle in Gilead?'). Alice would have known about this, not least because one of the illuminated windows in Christ Church, designed by Sir Edward Burne-Jones in 1860 and devoted to St Frideswide, has a panel depicting pilgrims going to the saint's healing well at Binsey near Oxford.

Of course, whether Alice knew that the rector of Binsey (from 1857) Thomas John Prout, was known for dozing off in college staff meetings – Binsey was, and is, part of the Christ Church estates – and might have been the model for the Dormouse is not certain. But we do know that stuffing a dormouse into a teapot was *not* so nonsensical: a teapot made a good place for a pet dormouse's nest.

Perhaps the most daring, or mischievous, characterization in *Wonderland* is of the Mock Turtle's Drawling-master, who was 'an old congar-eel, that used to come once a week: *he* taught us Drawling, Stretching, and Fainting in Coils.'[13] This is almost certainly a reference to John Ruskin, who graduated as gentleman commoner from Christ Church in 1836. Dodgson counted him as a friend, and he tutored Alice Liddell for a time (very effectively, to judge from her paintings). By 1865, Ruskin was a powerful figure, with much of his most famous work, *The Stones of Venice* (1851), *Unto this Last* (1860) and his contribution to the founding of the Oxford Natural History Museum (1860) behind him. His influence as an art critic is demonstrated by this squib published in *Punch* on 24 May 1856 by Shirley Brooks (who became its editor in 1870):

> I paints and paints
> Hears no complaints
> And sells before I'm dry,
> Till savage Ruskin
> He sticks his tusk in
> Then nobody will buy.

Some of the caricatures of the youngish Ruskin certainly support the congar-eel image, but this joke must have carried a certain *frisson* for the Deanery children.

We have seen how Dodgson parodied the verses that Alice and her sisters would have learned to recite. Not all of these were initially directed at children, such as the American David Bates's 'Speak Gently' (1845):

> Speak gently! – It is better far
> To rule by love, than fear –
> Speak gently – let not harsh words mar
> The good we might do here!

GREAT GUNS OF OXFORD. *President of the Amateur Landscape Gardening Society*.

John Ruskin, Slade Professor of Fine Art, friend of the Liddells and Alice's sometime drawing – or 'drawling' – tutor, had wide social interests. The Shrimptons' cartoon (c.1874) lampoons his involvement in the North Hinksey road improvement scheme.

Speak gently! – Love doth whisper low
The vows that true hearts bind;
And gently Friendship's accents flow;
Affection's voice is kind.

Speak gently to the little child!
Its love be sure to gain;
Teach it in accents soft and mild: –
It may not long remain.

When Alice enters the Duchess's kitchen – itself a parody of all comfortable and comforting literary kitchens – this re-emerges as a verse whose third and fourth lines have become proverbial in many British households:

Speak roughly to your little boy,
And beat him when he sneezes:
He only does it to annoy,
Because he knows it teases.[14]

Some of the parodies are very local indeed. In *Under Ground* (although not in *Wonderland*) the Mock Turtle sings a version of a song which, as Dodgson notes in his diary (2 July 1862), the three Liddell sisters sang after lunch at the Deanery, 'with great spirit'. Originally it began

Sally come up, Oh, Sally come down,
Oh Sally, come twist your heels around.

And, not unnaturally, the Mock Turtle comes out with

Salmon come up! Salmon go down!
Salmon come twist your tail around![15]

Similarly, on 1 August 1862, Dodgson heard Alice and Edith sing the Christy Minstrel song 'Beautiful Star' (1855):

Beautiful star in heav'n so bright
Softly falls thy silv'ry light,
As thou movest from earth so far,
Star of the evening, beautiful star.
  Beau—ti-ful star,
  Beau—ti-ful star,

Star-r of the eve-ning,
Beautiful, beautiful star.

The same parody appears in *Under Ground* and *Wonderland*, sung by the Mock Turtle 'in a voice choked with sobs':

Beautiful Soup, so rich and green,
Waiting in a hot tureen!
Who for such dainties would not stoop?
Soup of the evening, beautiful Soup!
Soup of the evening, beautiful Soup!
   Beau—ootiful Soo—oop
   Beau—ootiful Soo—oop!
Soo-oop of the e-e-evening,
   Beautiful Soup![16]

There is a story that when *real* turtle soup was on the menu at Christ Church, the children were allowed to ride the turtles in the kitchens.

It is striking that, when Dodgson came to assemble *Looking-Glass*, and he had, in real life, little to do with the growing Liddell children, there is only one brief parody, of 'Rock-a-bye baby': this element of childhood was no longer so relevant. And although the Alice character is clearly intended to be the same character as in *Wonderland* there are very few direct references to their mutual experience. Alice's younger sisters, Rhoda (b. 1859) and Violet (b. 1864) make a brief appearance in the Garden of Live Flowers; the chess game itself may reflect the games Dodgson played with the Liddells; the chessboard pattern of countryside viewed from the little hill may reflect a

By 1890, when John Tenniel supervised the revision and simplification of some of his original illustrations for *The Nursery Alice*, fashions had changed, and Alice acquired a pleated skirt and a hair-ribbon.

visit to Charlton Kings – where there is a notable looking-glass in the house in which the Liddells stayed. Similarly, the interest that the White King has in troop movements may reflect a mutual memory, that the day before the mythic boat trip, the marriage of Edward, Prince of Wales was marked by a 'Celebrity Battle' featuring hundreds of volunteers on Christ Church meadow.

> 'Did you happen to meet any soldiers, my dear, as you came through the wood?'
> 'Yes I did,' said Alice: 'several thousand, I should think.'
> 'Four thousand two hundred and seven, that's the exact number,' the King said, referring to his book.'[17]

But, as time went on, there is a gradual shift in the books from a preoccupation with experiences shared by Alice, her sisters and Dodgson, to the preoccupations of Dodgson's highly individual mind.

Another example from the first version of Butcher's slide set of *Alice in Wonderland*: the set was later redrawn, possibly because of high demand, with the loss of many details.

4
OUTSIDE CHARLES DODGSON

'Somehow it seems to fill my head with ideas – only I don't exactly know what they are!' – Alice on 'Jabberwocky'[1]

Dodgson was such an indefatigable and pugnacious satirist, peppering Christ Church and Oxford with witty, and often anonymous, pamphlets, that it is hardly surprising that he packed the 'Alice' books with scurrilous material. Here was a perfect stalking-horse: the innocent children's book. Kingsley might have proclaimed his prejudices in *The Water Babies* and by doing so destroyed the magic of the tale: Dodgson was much subtler and much more introspective. And, as with many ironists, it did not matter to him if he was the only one who got the joke.

The problem for readers now, of course, is to unravel the accidental from the intentional: for an example, let us return to the Mad Tea-Party. The episode does not occur in *Under Ground* and it is tempting to see it as a satire on what became widely known (as it made the national papers) as the 'Bread and Butter War'. Dodgson and his friend Thomas Prout led a campaign through 1864 (aimed ultimately at Dean Liddell) to improve the standard of food in Christ Church by reforming the system by which the college servants made what profit they could from providing food and drink. The illogic, injustice and general mayhem of the tea-party seem like an apt description of what was going on in real life:

'I want a clean cup,' interrupted the Hatter: 'let's all move one place on.'

He moved on as he spoke, and the Dormouse followed him: the March Hare moved into the Dormouse's place, and Alice rather unwillingly took the place of the March Hare. The Hatter was the only one who got any advantage from the change …[2]

Given that it is tempting to see Dr Prout as the Dormouse, was Dodgson lampooning others involved? Scholars have suggested two then well-known Oxford characters as candidates for the role of the Hatter – Theophilus Carter, inventor of the alarm clock bed, and Thomas Randall, hatter and Mayor of Oxford, whose daughter, Eliza, was a friend of the Liddells. However, whereas there is no evidence that Tenniel ever came to Oxford to sketch either of them, he had only to look at images of Dean Liddell to find a model. (The March Hare could have been a reference to Julius Charles Hare (1795–1855), Archdeacon of Lewes, who supported Kingsley and his broad church socialist ideas, but this does not fit very neatly into the bread-and-butter theory!)

Another controversial broad church figure to whose extensive University reforms Dodgson strongly objected – indeed, he made his only speech in Congregation (the University's 'Parliament') in 1861 on the issues – was Benjamin Jowett. An imposing figure, Jowett was the subject of a student squib:

Here come I, my name is Jowett
There is no knowledge but I know it
I am the master of this college
What I don't know isn't knowledge.

In *Wonderland*, Alice finds herself reciting to the Caterpillar – drawn by Tenniel with the sleeves of an academic gown. She attempts Robert Southey's 'The Old Man's Comforts and How He Gained Them' (*Annual Anthology* 1, 1799):

Ecclesiastical madness? The Dean of Christ Church (the Hatter) addresses the Archdeacon of Lewes (the March Hare), the Rector of Binsey (the Dormouse), and his own daughter.

You are old, Father William, the young man cried,
 The few locks which are left you are grey;
You are hale, Father William, a hearty old man,
 Now tell me the reason I pray.
In the days of my youth, Father William replied,
 I remember'd that youth would fly fast,
And abused not my health and my vigour at first
 That I never might need them at last.

Oxford as the centre of artistic and philosophical debate: John Ruskin and Benjamin Jowett on opposite sides of the 'Temple of Truth'. Another squib from the Shrimptons' 'Oxford Caricatures', c.1872.

(Robert Southey, Poet Laureate 1813–43, was Samuel Taylor Coleridge's brother-in-law, a friend of Thomas Telford of Menai Bridge fame, and revived the story of Goldilocks.)

Alice's unfortunate attempt (backed up by Tenniel's illustration, which can easily be seen as a caricature) might well be a muted attack on Jowett:

76

The arrogant (and possibly high) academic caterpillar. Could this be Dr Jowett, Master of Balliol, one of whose *obiter dicta* was 'Never retreat. Never explain. Get it done and let them howl.'

'You are old, Father William,' the young man said,
  'And your hair has become very white;
And yet you incessantly stand on your head –
  Do you think, at your age, it is right?'

'In my youth,' Father William replied to his son,
  'I feared it might injure the brain;
But, now that I'm perfectly sure I have none,
  Why, I do it again and again.'[3]

But more universal issues than University reforms were being debated, and Dodgson, a high church man with some socialist sympathies and an acute sense of humour, was naturally drawn into them – which brings us to the puppy.

In Chapter III of *Under Ground*, and Chapter IV of *Wonderland*, in virtually the same words, Alice, three inches tall, meets an enthusiastic puppy:

> An enormous puppy was looking down at her with large round eyes, and feebly stretching out one paw, trying to touch her. 'Poor little thing!' said Alice, in a coaxing tone, and she tried hard to whistle to it; but she was terribly frightened all the time at the thought that it might be hungry, in which case it would be very likely to eat her up in spite of all her coaxing.
>
> Hardly knowing what she did, she picked up a little bit of stick and held it out to the puppy: whereupon the puppy jumped into the air off all its feet at once, with a yelp of delight, and rushed at the stick, and made to worry it: then Alice dodged behind a great thistle, to keep herself from being run over; and the moment she appeared on the other side, the puppy made another rush at the stick, and tumbled head over heels in its hurry to get hold of it.

All very innocent, we might think, and an ordinary sort of device for a fantasy where the female hero is changing size all the time.

Except for the fact that on 30 June 1860 there was a famous, or notorious, meeting of the British Association for the Advancement of Science at the new Oxford Museum. This turned into a debate between, among others, Thomas Huxley, an apologist for Charles Darwin (who was ill), and Samuel Wilberforce, Bishop of Oxford (aka Soapy Sam because of his sometimes slippery rhetoric), on Darwin's newly published theories of natural selection. These theories were a cultural turning point, producing a conflict between the infallibility of Holy Writ and the idea that Man was not God's last word and might have descended from the apes in an endless evolutionary process. The implications of this, especially for established religion, were monumental

One of John Tenniel's original drawings for 'You are old, Father William', Dodgson's parody of Southey. The eel-weir in the background draft consisted of wicker baskets to catch eels, and Alice would have seen them on her picnics with Dodgson in Godstow backwater. This is the mirror image of the published picture, before it was engraved by the Dalziel Brothers.

– and not least for children's books, where the certainties of religious reward and punishment were particularly embedded. The debate was swung by a contribution from Joseph Dalton Hooker, a close friend of Darwin.

In the audience – having spent the large sum of two guineas for a ticket – was Charles Dodgson. He had a certain personal involvement, having been ordained by Wilberforce, whom he had also photographed.

And the puppy? Certainly Dodgson's original illustration in *Under Ground* is of an all-purpose puppy, but something curious happens when it comes to Tenniel's illustration for *Wonderland*. Tenniel, it must not be forgotten, was above all a political cartoonist and caricaturist, and the face of his puppy certainly seems to be familiar.

Could it be the young Charles Darwin? And could the rest of the dog be a beagle – then a rather differently shaped dog from the present breed (and, of course, Darwin's scientific career was based on his five-year voyage in HMS *Beagle*)? Or, then again, is it Thomas Huxley, who was known as 'Darwin's Bulldog', and who mounted such an ineffectual, but memorable, defence of Darwin at the lecture? (Dodgson took a photograph of Huxley later.) This particular satirical jab may have found its mark – Darwin's son claimed that of all the personal attacks on him, Darwin was most hurt by being described as a dog!

If this seems a little fanciful, there are two other clues to Dodgson's playfulness. Can it be a coincidence that Alice took refuge behind a 'great

Could there be a resemblance? Alice and the boisterous puppy – and Charles Darwin in 1849, aged 40.

thistle', and one of Dodgson's colleagues at Oxford was William Turner Thiselton-Dyer (1843–1928)? He studied mathematics at Christ Church, and then moved on to natural sciences – and was not at that point a Darwinist. Who better might Alice shelter behind to eacape from this bouncy Darwin–Huxley creature? The second is the fact that both Dodgson's and Tenniel's illustrations of the pool of tears (perhaps the primordial fluid?) include – incongruously among the domestic animals and birds – an ape.

Dodgson's approach to this controversy differed from that of Margaret Gatty or Charles Kingsley. Gatty, in *Parables from Nature*, had directly challenged what she saw as Darwin's arrogance and materialism; Kingsley, in *The Water Babies*, had attempted to develop a new fusion between religion and science – the chimney sweep Tom evolves from being a 'little black ape' to a 'great man of science'. Dodgson faced the ambiguities of the new world. In the caucus race, Alice's changing size and shape, the baby changing into a pig, the doomed looking-glass insects, and the fact that human superiority over animals is constantly undermined and nature is uninterested in Alice's survival, Dodgson is making a point about the post-Darwinian, godless universe. This is a world of the survival of the fittest: everything is unstable and threatening; pious verses become savage, and Alice survives not by reason or authority, but by her passive–aggressive behaviour. What has seemed – and seems – to many to be a liberal, liberating image of childhood is in fact a post-Darwinian nightmare. It may be that the fact that it is all, in the end, only a dream, is not a failure of feminist nerve on Dodgson's part, or an admission of the reality of the position of the girl-child in society, but a desperate hope that things will *not* change.

Of course, we may be barking up the wrong thistle, and the puppy might be a merely cheerful dig at Charles Kingsley, who Thomas Hughes (author of *Tom Brown's Schooldays*) described as being like a Newfoundland puppy bouncing along after every new enthusiasm.

Even the Mad Tea-Party may be unpolitical – and a lot nearer plain reality than one might suppose. In 1863, Dodgson, in his quest for celebrity photographs, had visited Dante Gabriel Rossetti in the somewhat unconventional household at 16 Cheyne Walk, London. Residents and visitors included James McNeill Whistler, William Morris, Algernon Charles Swinburne, George Meredith, Ford Madox Brown, and the notorious blackmailer Charles Augustus Howell. There were riotous dinner parties – and 'also Rossetti's menagerie. A wombat slept contentedly on the dining-table. An armadillo and a kangaroo lived in the gardens'.[4]

Dodgson photographed the Rossetti family, including Christina, and wrote to her praising her *Goblin Market* (1862). Although that poem's perfervid sensuality may disqualify it as a children's book, a reflection of it may survive in *Looking-Glass*, when Alice plunges her arms 'elbow-deep' into the stream to pick 'one bunch after another of the darling scented rushes'.[5]

> Laura stretch'd her gleaming neck
> Like a rush-imbedded swan,
> Like a lily from the beck,
> Like a moonlit poplar branch,
> Like a vessel at the launch
> When its last restraint is gone.

Some of Dodgson's references to people are more obvious and more affectionate. The Hatter recalls a song that he sang 'at a concert given by the Queen of Hearts':

> '*"Twinkle, twinkle, little bat!*
> *How I wonder what you're at!"*

You know the song, perhaps?'
  'I've heard something like it,' said Alice.

'It goes on, you know,' the Hatter continued, 'in this way: –

"Up above the world you fly
Like a tea-tray in the sky … "'

This is, of course, a parody of Jane Taylor's 'The Star' from *Rhymes for the Nursery* (1806) which has survived into national idiom:

Twinkle, twinkle, little star,
How I wonder what you are!
Up above the world so high,
Like a diamond in the sky.

'Bat' was the nickname of Bartholomew Price, mathematical lecturer at Oxford from 1845, and Dodgson attended a reading party with him at Whitby in the summer of 1854.

But all of this is, in a sense, the public face of Dodgson: the 'Alice' books were made of much more of the fabric of his mind, logical and mathematical on one hand, and deeply sentimental on the other.

The great and the good: Dodgson had read them, knew them or photographed them, and in at least three cases satirized them in the 'Alice' books. A plate from *English Celebrities of the Nineteenth Century* (1876). Back row, l to r: John Stewart Mill, Charles Kingsley, Charles Darwin; Front row, l to r: Charles Lamb, Herbert Spenser, John Ruskin.

5

INSIDE CHARLES DODGSON

'You are sad,' the Knight said in an anxious tone: 'let me sing you a song to comfort you.'

'Is it very long?' Alice asked, for she had heard a good deal of poetry that day.

'It's long,' said the Knight, 'but it's very, very beautiful. Everybody that hears me sing it – either it brings the tears into their eyes, or else –'

'Or else what?' said Alice, for the Knight had made a sudden pause.

'Or else it doesn't, you know …'[1]

One of the key features of the 'Alice' books is the *respect* which Dodgson showed for his child readers. As we have seen, it did not matter to him whether the jokes were ever deciphered (which has, of course, led to a good deal of deciphering), but when it came to chess, or mathematics or logic, he seems to have assumed that he was addressing his peers.

Examples abound. At the beginning of *Wonderland* when the fictional Alice is trying to work out who she is, she tries geography ('Paris is the capital of Rome'), poetry ('How doth the little crocodile …'), and the times table:

'Let me see: four times five is twelve, and four times six is thirteen, and four times seven is – oh dear! I shall never get to twenty at that rate!'[2]

It is no surprise that, mathematically, this is not nonsense, because if Alice continues in this progression to 'twelve times twelve', the usual end of the times table, the final number is 19. This is because 4×5 *is* 12 in a number sequence using base 18, and 4 × 6 *is* 13 using base 21 – but that that progression breaks down when we reach (or don't reach) 20. Dodgson's delight in this kind of ingenuity seems to be obvious.

And then there is the number 42, which Dodgson seems to have, shall we say, taken a lifelong interest in.

> At this moment the King, who had been for some time busily writing in his note-book, called out 'Silence!', and read out from his books, 'Rule Forty-two. *All persons more than a mile high to leave the court*. ... It's the oldest rule in the book.'
> ... 'Then it ought to be Number One,' said Alice.[3]

Wonderland has forty-two illustrations, and *Looking-Glass*, which now has fifty, was originally announced as having forty-two. Perhaps it is a coincidence that in *Looking-Glass*, the King sends 4,207 horses (7 is a factor of 42), but the conversation that Alice has with the White Queen seems to leave little doubt that we are dealing with an extraordinarily devious mind.

It has been established that in *Looking-Glass* Alice's age is seven years and six months, and that the book is set on 4 November 1859. The White Queen, questioning Alice in the best governess style, says

> 'Let's consider your age to begin with – how old are you?'
> 'I'm seven and a half, exactly.'
> 'You needn't say "exactually,"' the Queen remarked. 'I can believe it without that. Now I'll give *you* something to believe. I'm just one hundred and one, five months and a day.'[4]

Now the fact that the elements of Alice's age, 7 and 6, when multiplied together, make 42 might be regarded as whimsically fortuitous. But a (remarkable) scholar, Edward Wakeling, has worked out that if you count the days that the White Queen has been alive, up to 4 November 1859 – not

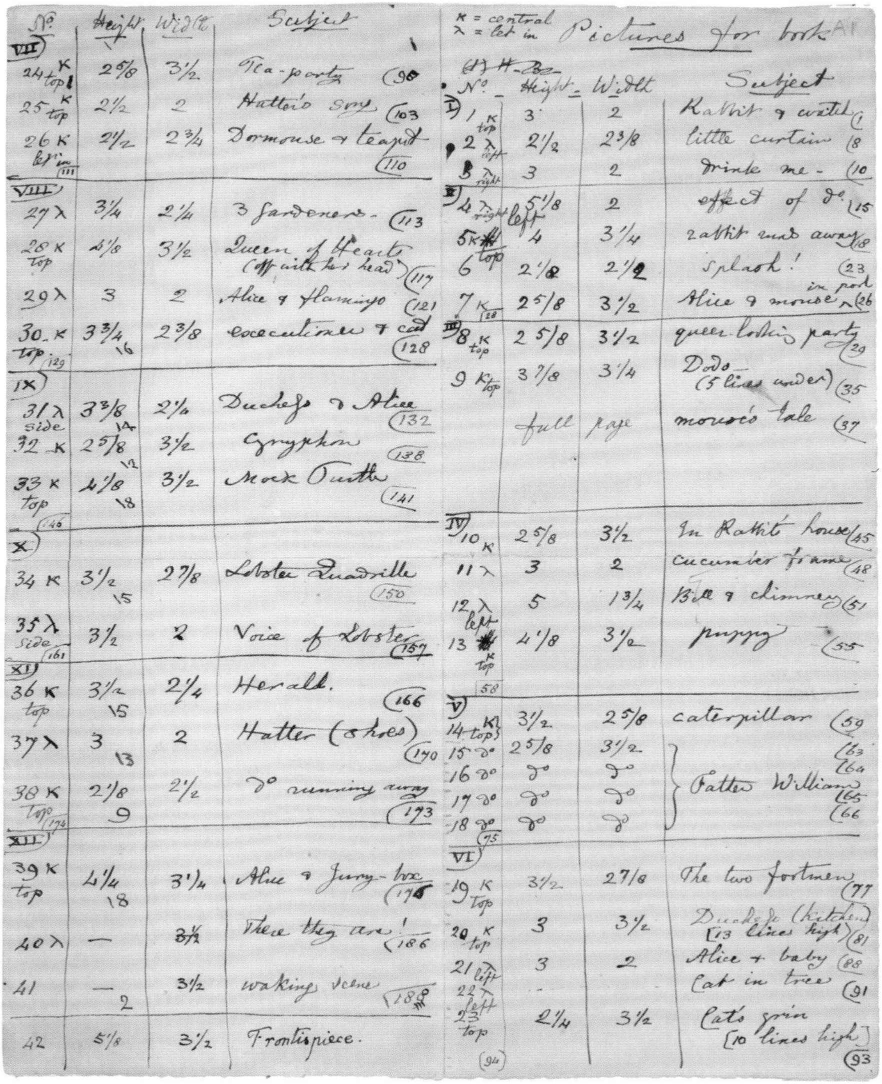

No.	Height	Width	Subject
VII			
24 κ top	2 5/8	3 1/2	Tea-party (98
25 κ top	2 1/2	2	Hatter's song (103
26 κ let in (111	2 1/2	2 3/4	Dormouse & teapot (110
VIII			
27 λ	3 1/4	2 1/4	3 gardeners (113
28 κ top	4 1/8	3 1/2	Queen of Hearts (off with her head) (117
29 λ	3	2	Alice & flamingo (121
30 κ top (129	3 3/4 16	2 3/8	executioner & cat (128
IX			
31 λ side	3 3/8 14	2 1/4	Duchess & Alice (132
32 κ	2 5/8 12	3 1/2	Gryphon (138
33 κ top (146	4 1/8 18	3 1/2	Mock Turtle (141
X			
34 κ	3 1/2 15	2 7/8	Lobster Quadrille (150
35 λ side (161	3 1/2	2	Voice of Lobster (157
XI			
36 κ top	3 1/2 15	2 1/4	Herald. (166
37 λ	3 13	2	Hatter (shoes) (170
38 κ top (174	2 1/8 9	2 1/2	do running away (173
XII			
39 κ top	4 1/4 18	3 1/4	Alice & Jury-box (178
40 λ	—	~~3 1/2~~	There they are! (186
41	— 2	3 1/2	waking scene (188
42	5/8	3 1/2	Frontispiece.

κ = central
λ = let in

Pictures for book

No.	Height	Width	Subject
I			
1 κ top	3	2	Rabbit & watch (7
2 λ left	2 1/2	2 3/8	little curtain (8
3 λ right	3	2	drink me (10
II			
4 λ right left	5 1/8	2	effect of do (15
5 κ top	4	3 1/4	rabbit runs away (18
6	2 1/8	2 1/2	splash! (23
7 κ (28	2 5/8	3 1/2	Alice & mouse in pool (26
III			
8 κ top	2 5/8	3 1/2	queer-looking party (29
9 κ top	3 7/8	3 1/4	Dodo (5 lines under) (35
	full	page	mouse's tale (37
IV			
10 κ	2 5/8	3 1/2	In Rabbit's house (45
11 λ	3	2	cucumber frame (48
12 λ left	5	1 3/4	Bill & chimney (51
13 κ top (58	4 1/8	3 1/2	puppy (55
V			
14 κ top	3 1/2	2 5/8	caterpillar (59
15 do	2 5/8	3 1/2	Father William (63
16 do	do	do	(64
17 do	do	do	(65
18 do (75	do	do	(66
VI			
19 κ top	3 1/2	2 7/8	The two footmen (77
20 κ top	3	3 1/2	Duchess (kitchen) [13 lines high] (81
21 left	3	2	Alice & baby (88
22 λ left	-		Cat in tree (91
23 top (94	2 1/4	3 1/2	Cat's grin [10 lines high] (93

On 25 January 1864, Dodgson met Tenniel in London and asked him to illustrate *Wonderland*; on 5 April, Tenniel agreed to do so; on 13 October, he showed Dodgson the first picture, and they agreed on 'about 34 pictures', which were all completed by 18 June, 1865. Tenniel was a very busy man.

forgetting leap years – the total is 37,044: double that (there are two Queens, and as they are in the same set, they must be the same age) – which makes 74,088 – and 74,088 just happens (?) to be 42 x 42 x 42.[5]

Even allowing for the complexity of Dodgson's thinking, there is an obvious danger that, like conspiracy theorists, we may see ingenuity in every line.

Take the (disputed) fact that in *Looking-Glass*, a book about a chess game in which the pieces are (as was common in the nineteenth century) red and black, the word "white" occurs 68 times, and the word "red" 68 times. This is, given what we know of Dodgson, not especially surprising – but why should he do it? Balance? (Incidentally, it seems that the modern game of chess was referred to as 'mad queen chess' from the fifteenth century.) And why 68? Of course, almost any number has mathematical and symbolic significance, and so it might be dangerous to read too much into this – but 68 does seem to have the kinds of attributes that would have appealed to Dodgson's mind. Mathematicians tell us that 68 is

- a 'happy number' – that is, if the numbers 6 and 8 are squared (= 36 and 64) and added together they make 100, and if the squares of 1, 0 and 0 are added together, they make 1;
- it is the largest even number that can be expressed in two ways as the sum of two prime numbers (7 + 61 = 31 + 37);
- it is not until the 606th and 607th digits of *pi* that the combination 68 appears (every other two-digit combination occurs earlier);
- and, especially, it is the number of squares accessible for three knight's moves, if the chessboard were big enough.

But, of course, that is not all. It is also the opus number of Beethoven's 6th Symphony, the 'Pastoral', and it is not stretching possibility too far to wonder whether Dodgson was parodying Beethoven's descriptions of its five movements in certain chapters in *Looking-Glass*.

1: 'Erwachen heiterer Empfindungen bei der Ankunft auf dem Lande' (*Awakening of Cheerful Feelings on Arriving in the Country*) – 'The Garden of Live Flowers';

2: 'Szene am Bach' (*Scene by the Brook*) – 'Looking-Glass Insects';

3: 'Lustiges Zusammensein der Landleute' (*Happy Gathering of Rustic People*) – 'Tweedledum and Tweedledee';

4: 'Gewitter, Sturm' (*Thunder, Storm*) – the crow in 'Tweedledum and Tweedledee' and 'Wool and Water' – and there is no pause between the third and fourth movements of the symphony, plus the third 'ends' with an imperfect (positively crow-like) cadence; and

5: 'Hirtengesang. Frohe und dankbare Gefühle nach dem Sturm' (*Shepherd's Song; Merry and Thankful Feelings after the Storm*) – 'Wool and Water'.

And, obviously, Dodgson was familiar with Beethoven: the 23rd of his 'Concrete Propositions' in *Symbolic Logic* reads:

(1) Nobody, who really appreciates Beethoven, fails to keep silence while the Moonlight-Sonata is being played;

(2) Guinea-pigs are hopelessly ignorant of music;

(3) No one, who is hopelessly ignorant of music, ever keeps silence while the Moonlight-Sonata is being played.

Equally, he might have been (wistfully) constructing another private joke for Alice Liddell and her sisters: Robert Schumann's *Album für die Jugend*, or *Album for the Young* (opus 68!) might well have been on a music stand in the Deanery. And the names of some of its eighteen pieces for children could be seen to be illustrated in *Looking-Glass*: 'Soldiers' march', 'The poor orphan', 'The wild horseman', 'First loss', and 'Little morning wanderer'.

And this is to ignore the fact that Carroll's father died in 1868 – the year he began the elegaic *Looking-Glass*.

Alice Liddell, probably in her early twenties: from a *carte de visite* photograph. Possibly because she had been tutored by Ruskin, she was a more-than-competent artist, especially with watercolour landscapes and humourous sketches.

Dodgson, among much else, has created an endless labyrinth.

But this is nothing compared to the labyrinth that he created in infusing his personal feelings into the books – and one way that he seems to have done this is by cameo appearances. One of the most subtle is the picture of Humpty Dumpty shouting into the ear of an anonymous character – his *right* ear: Dodgson was deaf … in his right ear. Probably the most curious is his turn as the Knave of Hearts (scarcely a subtle disguise, given his strong feelings for his child friends). The trial of the Knave is based on the old rhyme (first recorded in 1792):

> The Queen of Hearts she made some tarts
> > All on a summer day:
> The Knave of Hearts he stole those tarts,
> > And took them right away!

The nineteenth century was the era of the sensation novel, books which sold in their millions, and occasionally rose to the level of respectable literature – such as Wilkie Collins' *The Woman in White* (1859–60) and M.E. Braddon's *Lady Audley's Secret* (1862). Their convoluted plots, packed with innuendo, are thoroughly lampooned here in verses which Dodgson had first written in 1855:

> *They told me you had been to her,*
> > *And mentioned me to him:*
> *She gave me a good character,*
> > *But said I could not swim.*
>
> *He sent them word I had not gone*
> > *(We know it to be true):*
> *If she should push the matter on,*
> > *What would become of you?*[6]

No little detail overlooked: the right ear is the right ear – Dodgson was deaf in his right ear. Humpty Dumpty shouting nonsense: 'I said it very loud and clear / I went and shouted in his ear.'

Many biographers have read these lines not merely as a satire on a singularly risible genre, but as a disguised, even passionate, protest against damaging rumours that may have been swirling around Oxford concerning Dodgson and the Liddells.

It might seem to some readers that we are now sailing dangerously close to intrusive speculation about Dodgson's private life, but in *Looking-Glass* his intentions could not have been made more clear. The opening and closing verses are hardly the cheerful, light-hearted verses one might expect; the first is all sadness and nostalgia for the lost world of *Wonderland*, and begins:

Scrambled symbolism: is Humpty Dumpty the ultimate pompous academic, or the corpulent railway king, George Hudson, about to fall into bankruptcy, or another disguise for Dodgson's song to lost love? Illustration from *Through the Looking-Glass*.

CHILD of the pure unclouded brow
　　And dreaming eyes of wonder!
Though time be fleet, and I and thou
　　Are half a life asunder,
Thy loving smile will surely hail
The love-gift of a fairy-tale.

And after a gloomy view of adulthood and death, it ends with the blunt inclusion of Alice Liddell's middle name:

> And, though the shadow of a sigh
>   May tremble through the story,
> For 'happy summer days' gone by,
>   And vanish'd summer glory --
> It shall not touch, with breath of bale,
> The pleasance of our fairy tale.

This does not seem to have much to do with childhood, and has a lot to do with Dodgson's sense of loss. Things become even more explicit in the final poem in *Looking-Glass*, the first letters of each line of which spell out Alice Pleasance Liddell:

> A BOAT, beneath a sunny sky
> Lingering onward dreamily
> In an evening of July –
>
> Children three that nestle near,
> Eager eye and willing ear ...

And it contains the unambiguous stanza:

> Still she haunts me, phantomwise,
> Alice moving under skies
> Never seen by waking eyes.

Given this unsubtle declaration, it seems reasonable to look at Dodgson's guest appearances in the *Looking-Glass* in a little more detail. There are three – the melancholy gnat who sighs himself away, Humpty Dumpty, and the White Knight. There was to be a fourth, a particularly dismal elderly wasp in a wig, but Tenniel, who, one suspects, could see what Dodgson was up to, drew the line at this – or rather, refused to draw the line. He wrote to Dodgson (1 June 1870): '… I am bound to say that the "wasp" character doesn't interest me in the least … I can't see my way to a picture. If you want to shorten the book … *there* is your opportunity.'

Humpty Dumpty, the pedantic logician, who for all his bravado is very delicate and is balanced precariously on a narrow (emotional) wall, recites a poem which begins

> *In winter, when the fields are white,*
> *I sing this song for your delight*

and includes the couplet

> *In summer, when the days are long,*
> *Perhaps you'll understand the song.*[7]

Which seems innocent enough, but it is a parody of a popular song that Alice Liddell would have been familiar with – Wathen Mark Wilks Call's 'Summer Days', which begins

> In summer when the days were long,
> We walked, two friends, in field and wood

but ends, rather more significantly

> In summer when the days are long,
> I love her as I loved of old;
> My heart is light, my step is strong,
> For love brings back those hours of gold,
> In summer, when the days are long.

Tenuous? Perhaps – but that cannot be said of one of the most elegiac passages in the whole of Victorian literature, the longest scene in either of the 'Alice' books.

Alice, on the brink of becoming a Queen in the chess game, is saved from the Red Knight by the White Knight. Could this be Dodgson taking his leave of Alice Liddell as she reaches maturity?

> 'It was a glorious victory, wasn't it?' said the White Knight, as he came up panting.
>
> 'I don't know,' Alice said doubtfully. 'I don't want to be anybody's prisoner. I want to be a Queen.'
>
> 'So you will, when you've crossed the next brook,' said the White Knight. 'I'll see you safe to the end of the wood – and then I must go back, you know. That's the end of my move.'

The White Knight is a man who invents eccentric things, makes up verses, is a great logician and linguistic pedant, has shaggy hair, and is generally helpless and hopeless. He also has habits of riding which seem curiously symbolic, even in pre-Freudian days. He falls off a great deal

> … and as he generally did this on the side on which Alice was walking, she soon found that it was the best plan not to walk *quite* close to the horse.
>
> 'I'm afraid you've not had much practice in riding,' she ventured to say, as she was helping him up from his fifth tumble.
>
> The Knight looked very much surprised, and a little offended at the remark. 'What makes you say that?' he asked, as he scrambled back into the saddle, keeping hold of Alice's hair with one hand, to save himself from falling over on the other side.
>
> 'Because people don't fall off quite so often, when they've had much practice.'

Many critics have seen the Knave of Hearts as a version of Dodgson, and his trial by gossip a reflection of his own life. Arthur Rackham's vision (*Alice's Adventures in Wonderland*, 1907) is suitably Kafkaesque.

'I've had plenty of practice,' the Knight said gravely: 'plenty of practice!' [and] … fell heavily on the top of his head exactly in the path where Alice was walking.

He offers to sing her a song (with a short logical diversion into what the name of the song *is called*, what the name of the song *is*, and what the *song* is). The tune is, the Knight claims, his own invention.

> So saying, he stopped his horse and let the reins fall on its neck: then, slowly beating time with one hand, and with a faint smile lighting up his gentle foolish face, as if he enjoyed the music of his song, he began.
>
> Of all the strange things that Alice saw in her journey Through The Looking-Glass, this was the one that she always remembered most clearly. Years afterwards she could bring the whole scene back again, as if it had been only yesterday – the mild blue eyes [Dodgson had blue eyes] and kindly smile of the Knight – the setting sun gleaming through his hair, and shining on his armour in a blaze of light that quite dazzled her – the horse quietly moving about, with the reins hanging loose on his neck, cropping the grass at her feet – and the black shadows of the forest behind – all this she took in like a picture, as, with one hand shading her eyes, she leant against a tree, watching the strange pair, and listening, in a half-dream, to the melancholy music of his song.
>
> 'But the tune *isn't* his own invention,' she said to herself: 'it's *"I give thee all, I can no more."*' She stood and listened very attentively, but no tears came into her eyes.[8]

'I give you all – I can no more' is the first line of a song by Thomas Moore, 'My Heart and Lute' – a popular ballad, which sums up a highly sentimental view of love and loss:

> I give thee all—I can no more
> Though poor the off'ring be;
> My heart and lute are all the store
> That I can bring to thee.

A lute whose gentle song reveals
The soul of love full well;
And, better far, a heart that feels
Much more than lute could tell.

Though love and song may fail, alas!
To keep life's clouds away,
At least 'twill make them lighter pass
Or gild them if they stay.
And ev'n if Care, at moments, flings
A discord o'er life's happy strain,
Let love but gently touch the strings,
'Twill all be sweet again!

(Incidentally, the music was by Sir Henry Rowley Bishop, who had been Professor of Music at Oxford; he also wrote 'There's No Place Like Home'.)

The scene reflects the Victorians' love of the chivalric side of romance, and the observation on the heartlessness of children is emphasized by the choice of the tune – one that would not have been lost on the now nineteen-year-old Alice Liddell.

As the Knight sang the last words of the ballad, he gathered up the reins, and turned his horse's head along the road by which they had come. 'You've only a few yards to go,' he said, 'down the hill and over that little brook, and then you'll be a Queen — But you'll stay and see me off first?' he added as Alice turned with an eager look in the direction to which he pointed. 'I sha'n't be long. You'll wait and wave your handkerchief when I get to that turn in the road! I think it'll encourage me, you see.'

'Of course I'll wait,' said Alice: 'and thank you very much for coming so far – and for the song – I liked it very much.'

'I hope so,' the Knight said doubtfully: 'but you didn't cry as much as I thought you would.'[9]

Many years later, Dodgson gave a home-made game to a child-friend, Olive Butler, and signed it 'from the White Knight. Nov. 21, 1892'.

One final, curious, and possibly unwarranted, connection here. It has often been pointed out that Tenniel's illustration of the White Knight resembles John Millais' painting, 'A Dream of the Past: Sir Isumbras at the Ford' (1857). In 1865 Dodgson had photographed Millais and his wife, Effie, who had previously been married to John Ruskin. Ruskin's only story for children, *The King of the Golden River – or the Black Brothers, a Legend of Stiria*, published (anonymously) in 1851, has the reputation of being the first fantasy written for a specific child. It was written in 1841, as Ruskin said, 'at the request of a very young lady, and solely for her amusement, without any idea of publication.' The child was Effie Gray, who was twelve – and Ruskin married her nine years later. The marriage was a short-lived disaster, possibly because, as several historians (and several scurrilous contemporaries) have suggested, Ruskin could not reconcile the real woman and the ideal woman.

Alice's hauntingly comic encounter with the White Knight may well be a sad satire on Millais' 'Sir Isumbras at the Ford' (1857), radiating security, as Sir Isumbras, on a black horse, carries the children across the river. (Ruskin, perhaps not surprisingly, described the picture as a 'catastrophe'.) Alice has to make her own way across the last brook.

If Dodgson ever considered eventually marrying one of his child-friends this may have been a lesson in being careful what you wish for.

It has been said that true nonsense must avoid the personal: once genuine feeling intrudes, then the spell is broken. For some readers this is what has happened with Dodgson, and this leaves, especially in *Looking-Glass*, an adult-centred narrative that seems out of place in what purports to be a children's book. However, because there is so little genuine nonsense in the books – almost every sentence, every action, as we have seen, has a perfectly sensible root – Dodgson was able to square the circle. His tough-minded fictional Alice, carrying the banner of independent childhood through worlds occupied by mad adults, who scarcely understand their own rules or their emotions, becomes fascinating to children and adults alike.

6

FROM OXFORD TO THE WIDE WORLD

If the careless writer … closes his book without marrying, or putting to death, or somehow disposing, not only of his principal personages, but of all who have acted a part in the drama above the degree of candle-snuffer, he creates an unsatisfied want in the minds of his readers … and they hardly part friends.
– Robert Bage, *Hermsprong, or Man as He Is Not* (1796)

The publication of *Looking-Glass* was (almost) the end of the 'making of' the books, but only the beginning of the making of a worldwide classic.

But before we follow the curious journey of all the 'Alice' books, it is fascinating to look at the careers of all the actors in the drama who we have met so far, 'after Alice'.

Christ Church, no mean character in itself, retains its academic and social eminence, although what the formidable Dean Liddell would have made of it now – almost as famous for being used as the model for the Great Hall at Hogwarts, of *Harry Potter* fame, by another major fantasy writer – is an interesting speculation. (As is what he would have made of the sermon preached by his successor jointly in honour of himself and Dodgson, who died four days before him.) Charles Dodgson's spacious apartments are now the Graduate Common Room.

In the boat on the Isis that day, apart from Dodgson and Alice, was the Duck. No ordinary duck, as it turned out. For Robinson Duckworth became a fellow of Trinity College, Oxford; from 1866 to 1870 he was instructor to Prince Leopold, Queen Victoria's youngest son, and proceeded thorough a royal career as Chaplain-in-Ordinary to Queen Victoria (1870). Later he visited Balmoral, and ministered to Edward VII (1910). By another coincidence, he officiated at the funeral of Charles Darwin. He died in 1911 and was buried in Westminster Abbey.

Then there were the Liddell sisters. Lorina, the eldest, married, not royally as her parents might have hoped, but respectably to a Fellow of All Souls, W.B. Skene of Hallyards and Pitlour, Fife, and lived in Scotland until her death in 1930. Edith – Tillie, the Eaglet – died when she was twenty-two, of peritonitis – Prince Leopold was a pallbearer at her funeral, and there is a memorial window by Burne-Jones in Christ Church dedicated to her.

Alice, who Dodgson described as 'one who was, through so many years, my ideal child-friend', was a talented painter, and (another entwined connection) carved a wooden door at St Frideswide's Church, Osney. She was last photographed by Dodgson in 1870; some biographers have tried to deduce all manner of emotional things from her gloomy, not to say sulky expression, but it was, simply, fashionable. There were rumours of a possible liaison with Prince Leopold – they were certainly friends, and there is a story that she gave him an accidental black eye during an unchaperoned trip to Iffley. But nothing came of it, and in 1880, in Westminster Abbey, she married another Christ Church man, Reginald Hargreaves (who played cricket for Hampshire) – although she did wear a brooch given to her by Leopold on her wedding dress.

It is some indication of the power of the 'Alice' legend that Mrs Hargreaves has had two full-length biographies written about her, although she appeared only three times on the literary stage. In 1885, Dodgson (always a shrewd marketer of his work) very deferentially persuaded her to allow a facsimile edition of *Under Ground* to be published. In later life, when she had lost her husband and two of her three sons (the third was named Caryl, although she denied any connection with Carroll), she sold the manuscript for the

In June 1868, Dodgson took over 'perhaps the largest College set [of rooms] in Oxford', ten rooms in the north-west corner of Tom Quad in Christ Church college, and lived there, when he was in Oxford, until his death. He commissioned the most famous ceramic artist of the Arts and Crafts movement, William De Morgan, to design the tiles around the fireplace, which feature exotic animals.

then record auction price of £15,000. (It was later purchased by a group of American collectors and returned to England.) Then, in 1932, at the Columbia University celebrations of the centenary of Dodgson's birth, she went to the USA and was feted by the American press and public.

And her fame has lived on. She was the subject of a film, Dennis Potter's *Dreamchild* (1985) with Ian Holm and Coral Browne; and John Logan's play *Peter and Alice* (2013, Noel Coward Theatre, London), which imagines a meeting between her and the inspiration for Peter Pan, John Llewelyn Davies (played by Judi Dench and Ben Whishaw).

The royal Duck: Robinson Duckworth DD CVO VD in 1889, soon to be Chaplain-in-Ordinary to Queen Victoria.

Another regular member of the boating expeditions was Mary Prickett, the Liddell girls' governess until 1871, who had a distinguished career in a different field. She married a successful wine merchant, Charles Foster, and became landlady of The Mitre, an Oxford coaching inn – perhaps *the* Oxford coaching inn – on the High Street. When she died, greatly respected, in 1920, her rooms were found to be full of photographs of the Liddell children.

The other members of the Liddell family have faded from (literary) public sight, although the younger achieved some distinction. The two flowers, Rhoda (1859–1949) and Violet (1864–1927) became OBE and MBE respectively;

of the boys, who did not appear in the books, Frederick (1865–1950) was knighted, and Lionel (1868–1942) was a British consul.

Among the supporting cast, there were some stellar performances. The twinkling Bat, Bartholomew Price, became master of Pembroke College, secretary of the Clarendon Press, and was Professor of Natural Philosophy until just before his death in December 1898. Perhaps equally spectacular was the career of the great thistle, Sir William Turner Thiselton-Dyer, who ended his career as Director of the Royal Botanic Gardens at Kew. Later in life he became a friend of Charles Darwin, who was one of his proposers when he was elected Fellow of the Royal Society. And he married Thomas Huxley's daughter, Harriet.

John Ruskin, the Drawling-master, continued his career as an eminent Victorian: in 1869 he became Slade Professor of Fine Art, a prominent anti-Darwinian, and a friend, in their later years, of Dean Liddell.

Even the Dormouse was awake enough to contribute to the story: the Revd Prout, as rector of Binsey, had St Margaret's Treacle Well restored – no doubt in response to the new interest in it by readers of 'A Mad Tea-Party'.

John Tenniel became Sir John Tenniel, and a very busy and even more highly regarded artist, so busy that the only project he collaborated with Dodgson on in later years was, as we shall see, *The Nursery 'Alice'*. (Rumour was that he found Dodgson so difficult to work with that he could not face doing another book.) He also, for ten years, sent an annual valentine to Elspeth Thompson – the future Mrs Kenneth Grahame.

And Charles Dodgson?

What happened to Dodgson has been the subject of at least fifteen biographies in English alone: and the answer is, more of the same, without Alice. He remained at Christ Church, and built a reputation as an amateur photographer: the studio that he had contrived on the roof of Christ Church in 1872 hosted royalty and many celebrities. He continued to be an avid

View from the Dean's Garden, Christ Church, by William Turner of Oxford (1789–1862).

theatregoer (and critic) and was a friend of Ellen Terry, the most famous actress of his day. He had many more 'child-friends' but gave up photographing them, or anyone else, in 1880, partly because of unseemly rumours.

After his father died, in 1868, he took his responsibilities as head of the family very seriously, and topped up the legacy that his father had left his unmarried sisters. His bank accounts show that he was very generous, notably to his one married sister, Mary Collingwood, and his cousins the Wilcoxes. They also show some oddities – at one point he paid one fifth of his income for six months to a mysterious Mr Foster with no explanation (his diary for that year has disappeared). He spent a lot of time looking after his family in Guildford (and nursing a sick nephew), and spent every summer in lodgings at Eastbourne.

In another display of generosity, he helped his cousin Elizabeth Georgina Wilcox publish *The Lost Plum-Cake*, and persuaded Macmillan to publish

When Alice's mother died in 1910, the *Oxford Journal Illustrated* published a family photograph with Mrs Liddell in the centre of the front row. Ina is on the end of the front row on the right, Alice on the end of the back row on the left. The two younger sisters, Violet and Rhoda, are third and second from the right on the back row. In 1920, Violet was invested as an MBE, and Rhoda as an OBE.

his friend William Synge's *Bumblebee Bongo's Budget*. Dodgson was for some time 'curator' of the Senior Common Room at Christ Church, with responsibility for buying considerable quantities of wine and other provisions – a post which generated reams of correspondence (and an orgy of minor squabbles). On one occasion, in 1889, he returned a box of 'Portugal fruit' to a wine merchant with the note: '[Mr Dodgson] would have thought it hardly necessary to point out that the Curator, whose duty it is to try to procure the *best* goods he can for Common Room, cannot possibly accept *presents* from any of the tradespeople concerned.' He contributed satirical pamphlets to a wide range of Oxford disputes, notably on *The New Belfry of Christ Church* (1872) – and to national issues. He contributed an article to *St James's Gazette* (22 July 1885) which was highly critical of the editor of the *Pall Mall Gazette*, W.T. Stead, not for his campaign against child prostitution, but because of the sensational way in which Stead reported it.

"—— you know you say things are 'much of a muchness';
did you ever see such a thing as a drawing of a muchness?"

ALICE IN WONDERLAND.

ALICE AND THE DORMOUSE.

Dodgson invested in railways and steamships, and from 1882 systematically contributed to over thirty charities. 'His main concern was for the ill, unprotected and vulnerable', and his charities included the Homes of Hope 'for fallen and friendless young women', the Metropolitan Association for Befriending Young Servants, and the Society for the Suppression of Vice.[1]

In 1876 came *The Hunting of the Snark*, generally regarded as a masterpiece of nonsense, but from then on his attitude to writing for children seems to have changed. He produced a facsimile of *Under Ground* in 1886, and continued to publish extensively in mathematics, not only as a professional mathematician, but also a series of puzzles or 'knots', 'A Tangled Tale', for Charlotte Yonge's *The Monthly Packet* in 1880. 'The writer's intention,' he wrote, 'was to embody in each Knot (like the medicine so dextrously, but ineffectually, concealed in the jam of our early childhood) one or more mathematical questions …'

This return to the didactic mode that had been conspicuously absent from the 'Alice' books was repeated, deliberately, in the two volumes of his long and highly eccentric novels *Sylvie and Bruno* (1889) and *Sylvie and Bruno Concluded* (1893). While there are flashes of the old style, the books hark back to the eccentric – and not child-centred – mode of *The Water Babies*, and they were not successful.

The same process seems to have been at work in Dodgson's final visit to the 'Alice' books, with *The Nursery 'Alice'*. The tone is set by the 'Preface' ('Addressed to Any Mother'):

… my ambition *now* is (is it a vain one?) to be read by Children aged from Nought to Five. To be read? Nay, not so. Say rather to be thumbed, to be

On 23 December 1886, *Alice in Wonderland, a Musical Dream Play, in Two Acts, for Children and Others* opened at the Prince of Wales Theatre in London. It was produced by Henry Savile Clarke, in close collaboration with Dodgson; Phoebe Carlo played Alice, and Dorothy d'Alcourt the Dormouse. 'As a whole,' Dodgson conceded, 'the play seems a success.'

cooed over, to be dogs'-eared, to be rumpled, to be kissed, by the illiterate, ungrammatical, dimpled Darlings that fill your Nursery with merry uproar.

The ending of the book is a fair sample of its style:

> And I think you'll *never* guess what happened next. The next thing was, Alice woke up out of her curious dream ... *Wouldn't* it be nice to have a curious dream, just like Alice?
>
> The best plan is this. First lie down under a tree, and wait till a White Rabbit runs by ... then shut your eyes, and pretend to be dear little Alice.
>
> Good-bye, Alice dear, good-bye.

But the old Dodgson is still with us: the book contains twenty illustrations by Tenniel (some redrawn) and a new cover illustration by E. Gertrude Thomson, which, of course, adds up to twenty-one – half the mystic number which features in his other books.

He died, on 14 January 1898, at his sisters' house, while working on the second volume of his *Symbolic Logic*.

From the outset *Wonderland* was a strong seller – by 1867 there were 10,000 copies in print; the first printing of *Looking-Glass* was 9,000 copies, and 15,000 had been sold by January 1872. By the time Dodgson asked Alice Liddell if he could produce a facsimile, *Wonderland* had sold 120,000. In 1886 came Henry Savile Clarke's stage version, and when Dodgson died *Wonderland* had reached 150,000 and *Looking-Glass* 100,000 copies. However, it is as well to note that this was not so remarkable: Hesba Stretton's *Jessica's First Prayer* (1867), a quintessential evangelical waif novel, had sold 1,500,000 by the end of the century.[2] In another part of the literary forest, G.A. Henty was selling 150,000 copies *a year* of his empire-building adventure stories.[3]

This is not quite the revolutionary change in children's literature that is sometimes claimed for the 'Alice' books, but there is no question that they

chini, na mikono imetokeza pembeni kwa juu.)

Kisha katika mfuatano wakapita Mawakili

kumi, wamepambwa kwa alama ya Huru Ka-rata, wakaenda wawili wawili kiaskari, halafu wakaja watoto wa Mfalme Mzunguwanne ku-

Curiouser and curiouser: one of hundreds of idiosyncratic translations, as the 'Alice' books spread across the world – 'Alice' in Swahili, in 1940. The Water Lily House in the background of Tenniel's original drawing has disappeared!

had an impact. Caroline Sigler notes that there were more than 200 Alice-inspired books published from 1860 to 1920; in fact, in an 1891 diary entry, Dodgson proposed making a collection of 'books of the *Alice* type'.[4] In 1889, in the 'Preface' to *Sylvie and Bruno* he reflected on this:

> I do not know if 'Alice in Wonderland' was an *original* story – I was, at least, no *conscious* imitator in writing it – but I do know that, since it came out, something like a dozen story-books have appeared, on identically the same pattern. The path I timidly explored – believing myself to be 'the first that ever burst into that silent sea' – is now a beaten high-road; all the way-side flowers have long ago been trampled into the dust …

However, some of the imitations, notably Christina Rossetti's *Speaking Likenesses* (1874), can be plausibly seen as a feminist riposte to the male-centred ideology embedded in the 'Alice' books.[5] Few, if any, of these imitators have survived to this day – possibly because most of them imitated the witty *manner*, rather than the complex and subversive *matter* of the books.

Nevertheless, the 'Alice' books rode a wave of fantasy literature for children, notably involving other worlds, which has lasted to this day: whether or not they *caused* the wave can be debated.

The first translations, *Alice's Abenteuer im Wunderland* and *Aventures d'Alice au pays des merveilles* were published in 1869 and since then, for all its quintessential Englishness, it has become a worldwide classic. In 2016, the 'definitive' study *Alice in a World of Wonderlands: The Translations of Lewis Carroll's Masterpiece* appeared, surveying 7,609 editions of *Wonderland* in 174 languages, and 1,530 of *Looking-Glass* in sixty-five languages and dialects, from Afrikaans to Zulu, via Cebuano, Ewondo, Ladino, Manlam Ngy, Papiamento and Uyghur – plus Cockney, Braille and Shorthand. It also includes well over a hundred back-translations of the Mad Tea-Party: for

The Bat twinkling at the Clarendon Press: Professor Bartholomew Price portrayed in Shrimpton's 'Oxford Caricatures' as 'An infinitesimal calculator', c.1875.

example, the Old English (West Saxon Dialect) translation *The Brave Deeds of Æthelgyth in Wonderland* features an "ale cup" twinkling in the sky.

And because it has become common currency, it has been adapted and adopted for every and any political, satirical and philosophical purpose. For example, 'Saki' produced 'The Westminster Alice' in *The Westminster Gazette* (1900–02), a comprehensive attack on both parties during the Boer War, and since then we have seen *Adolf in Blunderland*, *Alice in Holidayland*, *Alice in Beeland*, the American National Lampoon's *Alice's Adventures in Cambridge*,

Hubert von Herkomer succeeded John Ruskin as Slade Professor of Fine Art at Oxford, and painted this posthumous portrait of Dodgson in 1899.

Alice's Bad Hair Day, Dyslexic Wonderland, Alice ... in one syllable, Alice for the iPad ... and a pornographic musical.

Walt Disney had flirted with Alice from early in his career, beginning with the twelve-minute *Alice's Wonderland* in 1923 in which Alice visits a film studio and watches animations. This was followed by a series of around sixty 'Laugh-O-Gram Alice' shorts. The full-length animated feature, *Alice in Wonderland*, 'an adaptation of Lewis Carroll's The Adventures of Alice in Wonderland' as the title credits have it, released in 1951, was one of the four films that nearly bankrupted the company (the others were *Fantasia*, *Pinocchio* and *Bambi*), and it lost around a million dollars. Although it is generally regarded as one of the most inventive – the directors of each segment trying to outdo each other – and has the most songs of any Disney films, its very Englishness seems to have limited its appeal.

So far, so successful. The books had moved from those genuinely appreciated by children to common currency, and they have generated an almost unrivalled quantity of biographies and academic books and articles. We can read about Dodgson's health, look at his bank accounts, read his diaries and letters. Novelists have weighed in with riffs on his life, from Donald Thomas's *Belladonna: a Lewis Carroll Nightmare* (1983) in which Dodgson is blackmailed, to Katie Roiphe's *Still She Haunts Me* (2001), which fills in some of the biographical blanks. Even more ambitious, perhaps, is Richard Wallace's *Jack the Ripper: 'Light Hearted Friend'* (1996) which suggests that Dodgson should be put at the top of the suspects list.

We are a long way from the idyllic scene on the Isis: ideas of innocence and simple fun have been replaced with suspicion. It is not uncommon to find that the first association in many people's minds when the subject of the 'Alice' books crops up is with questionable aspects of Dodgson's character. Perhaps appropriately enough, this phenomenon can be traced back to a joke.

In 1933 an Oxford undergraduate, Tony Goldschmidt, wrote a satire on the excesses of fashionable Freudian analysis in *The New Oxford Outlook* – '*Alice in Wonderland* Psycho-Analysed'. 'Alice' turned out to be an easy target – underground tunnels, changes of size, pools of water – and Goldschmidt gleefully exploits them, ending with the cheerful opinion that if Dodgson had 'undergone analysis [he would have] discovered the cause of his neurosis, and lived a more contented life'.[6] All good fun, and it may well have been true, but it was all too tempting for certain critics. From then on, Dodgson's life was the focus: his photography of young girls, the mysterious missing parts of his diary – several volumes have disappeared, and others have been, literally, cut– all produced a perfect storm of speculation.[7] Was the photography of naked young girls a perfectly normal art form in Victorian England, or was Dodgson a paedophile, repressed or otherwise? Biographies have become the trial of Charles Dodgson: his portrayal of the trial of the Knave of Hearts becomes remarkably prescient. And yet the question is – as with the life of every author – is this material relevant or even interesting?

Similarly, and in a twist that might have amused Dodgson rather more, the search for disguised references, for sources and for Dodgson's playful allusions (as, for example, in this book) was started by an academic paper that might well itself have been a joke. In the same year as Goldschmidt's, Shane Leslie (Winston Churchill's cousin) delivered a paper at the University of Göttingen, 'Lewis Carroll and the Oxford Movement'. 'It is not profane to suggest,' he wrote, 'that *Alice in Wonderland* may contain a secret history of the Oxford Movement.'[8] As a sample, Leslie explained the clash between the Red Knight and the White Knight as Dodgson's parody of the 1866 meeting of the British Association:

> Alice … may be regarded as the simple freshman or everyman who wanders like a sweet and innocent undergraduate into the Wonderland of a Victorian Oxford when everybody was religious in some way or another … The White Knight represents Victorian science, or Huxley in his most cocksure and inventive mood. The Red Knight corresponding is his old enemy Bishop

It is hardly a surprise that Dodgson rejected the first 10,000 copies of *The Nursery 'Alice'* in 1889 because they were 'far too bright and gaudy', and two more sample printings before he approved the edition. Emily Gertrude Thomson, the cover artist, was a friend of Dodgson, and had illustrated William Allingham's 'The Faeries'; her style suited the very different tone of this version of 'Alice'.

THE NURSERY "ALICE"

E. G. Thomson—

Wilberforce, and they arrive in the same square together and both try to make a capture of Alice.[9]

Well, possibly.

And Dodgson might have been entertained by the comment from the American President Calvin Coolidge, who on learning that the first edition had been suppressed, exclaimed: 'I didn't know there was anything off-colour in *Alice*!'[10]

The 'Alice' books are double creatures: they are part of a private conversation, and the property of the world; they are the furniture of the mind of an eccentric Victorian Oxford scholar, and yet are pertinent to the wide world of the twenty-first century. Are they liberal or conservative, funny or sinister, delightful or despairing? Looking into the making of the books, once down the rabbit-hole we can only follow passages, open doors, chase rabbits: in effect, join in Charles Dodgson's games. How far we like what we find, or find what we like, whether it is the sunlight on the river or some darker undercurrents, may be entirely up to us.

NOTES

In the chapter references below, *Under Ground* refers to *Alice's Adventures Under Ground*, *Wonderland* to *Alice's Adventures in Wonderland* and *Looking-Glass* to *Through the Looking-Glass* – see the Further Reading for editions.

Prelude

1   Martin Gardner (ed.), *The Annotated Snark*, Penguin, Harmondsworth, 1974, p. 22.
2   Humphrey Carpenter, *Secret Gardens*, Unwin, London, 1987, p. 37.
3   F.J. Harvey Darton, *Children's Books in England*, third edn, Cambridge University Press, Cambridge, 1982, p. 260.
4   Derek Hudson, *Lewis Carroll. An Illustrated Biography*, Constable, London, 1954, p. 73.
5   Martin Gardner (ed.), *The Annotated Alice. The Definitive Edition*, W.W. Norton, New York, 2000, pp. xiv, xv.

Chapter 1

1   *Looking-Glass*, VI.
2   Quoted by Stuart Dodgson Collingwood, *The Lewis Carroll Picture Book*, T. Fisher Unwin, London, 1899, pp. 258, 260.
3   Ibid., p. 165.
4   Kenneth Grahame, *The Wind in the Willows*, Oxford University Press, Oxford, 2010 [1908], p. 133.
5   Collingwood, *Picture Book*, pp. 166–7.
6   *Looking-Glass*, I.
7   *Looking-Glass*, VI.
8   Charlie Lovett, *Lewis Carroll Among his Books. A Descriptive Catalogue*, McFarland, Jefferson, NC, 2005, p. 3.

Chapter 2

1   Lewis Carroll, 'Alice on the Stage', *The Theatre*, April 1887, in Collingwood, *Picture Book*, p. 165.
2   Humphrey Carpenter and Mari Prichard, *The Oxford Companion to Children's Literature*, Oxford University Press, Oxford, 1984, p. 17.
3   Darton, *Children's Books*, p. 260.
4   Robert Phillips, *Aspects of Alice*, Penguin, Harmondsworth, 1971, p. 119.
5   *Wonderland*, X.
6   Ibid., II.
7   Charles Lamb, *Collected Letters*, ed. E.V. Lucas, Methuen, London, 1935, p. 326.
8   Charles Dodgson, 'My Fairy', in *The Complete Illustrated Lewis Carroll*, Wordsworth Editions, Ware, 1996, p. 700.
9   *Wonderland*, I.
10 Ibid., IX.
11 Ibid., X
12 Morton N. Cohen, *Lewis Carroll. A Biography*, Macmillan, London, 1995. p. 80.
13 *Wonderland*, I.
14 *Looking-Glass*, IX.
15 See Horst Dölvers, *Fables Less and Less Fabulous: English Fables and Parables of the Nineteenth Century and their Illustrations,* University of Delaware Press, Cranbury, NJ, 1997.
16 See Richard Foulkes, *Lewis Carroll and the Victorian Stage. Theatricals in a Quiet Life*, Routledge, New York and London, 2017.
17 John Payne Collier, *Punch and Judy*, fifth edn, Bell and Daldy, London, 1879, p. 78 archive.org/details/punchjudy00colluoft [5 November 2018]
18 Chapter 7.
19 *Looking-Glass*, XIII.

Chapter 3

1 *Wonderland*, IV.
2 Ibid., I.
3 Ibid., II.
4 *Looking-Glass*, I.
5 *Wonderland*, I.
6 Arthur Ransome, *Missee Lee,* Jonathan Cape, London, 1941, p. 186.
7 *Wonderland*, II.
8 Ibid., I.
9 *Under Ground*, II.
10 See Mark J. Davies, *Alice in Waterland. Lewis Carroll and the River Thanes in Oxford*, Signal Books, Oxford, p. 79.
11 *Under Ground*, II.
12 *Wonderland*, VII.
13 Ibid., IX
14 *Wonderland*, VI.
15 Ibid., X.
16 Ibid., and *Under Ground*, IV.
17 *Looking-Glass*, VII.

Chapter 4

1 *Looking-Glass*, I.
2 *Wonderland*, VII.
3 *Wonderland*, V.
4 Donald Thomas, *Lewis Carroll: A Portrait with Background*, John Murray, London, 1996, pp. 185–6.
5 *Looking-Glass*, V.

Chapter 5

1 *Looking-Glass*, VIII.
2 *Wonderland*, II.
3 Ibid., XII.
4 *Looking-Glass*, V.

5 Jenny Woolf, *The Mystery of Lewis Carroll, Discovering the Whimsical, Thoughtful, and Sometimes Lonely Man who Created Alice in Wonderland*, St Martin's Press, New York, 2010, pp. 57–8.
6 *Wonderland*, XII.
7 *Looking-Glass*, VI.
8 *Looking-Glass*, VIII.
9 Ibid.

Chapter 6

1 Jenny Woolf, *The Mystery of Lewis Carroll*, pp. 285–6.
2 Jan Susina, *The Place of Lewis Carroll in Children's Literature*, Routledge, New York and London, 2010, p. 26.
3 Guy Arnold, *Held Fast For England: G.A. Henty, Imperialist Boys' Writer*, Hamish Hamilton, London, 1980, p. 17.
4 Carolyn Sigler (ed.), *Alternative Alices: Visions and Revisions of Lewis Carroll's Alice Books. An Anthology*, University Press of Kentucky, Lexington, KY, 1997, p. xi.
5 See U.L. Knoepflmacher, *Ventures into Childhood: Victorians, Fairy Tales, and Femininity,* University of Chicago Press, Chicago, 1998, pp. 352-70.
6 Phillips, *Aspects*, p. 332.
7 See, for example, Karoline Leach, *In the Shadow of the Dreamchild: The Myth and Reality of Lewis Carroll*, Peter Owen, London, 2009, pp. 193–6.
8 Phillips, *Aspects*, p. 257.
9 Ibid., pp. 258, 265.
10 Paul F. Boller, Jr. (ed.), *Presidential Anecdotes*, Penguin, Harmondsworth, 1982, p. 243.

FURTHER READING

Editions

Carroll, L., *Alice's Adventures Under Ground: A Facsimile*, British Library, London, 2008. www.bl.uk/collection-items/alices-adventures-under-ground-the-original-manuscript-version-of-alices-adventures-in-wonderland

Carroll, L., *The Nursery Alice*, Macmillan Children's Books, London, 2015.

Collingwood, S.D. (ed.), *The Lewis Carroll Picture Book*, T. Fisher Unwin, London, 1899. Subsequently reissued as *Diversions and Digressions of Lewis Carroll* and *The Unknown Lewis Carroll.* https://archive.org/details/lewiscarrollpict00carruoft

Gardner, M. (ed.), *The Annotated Alice: The Definitive Edition,* W.W. Norton, New York, 2000.

Hunt, P. (ed.), *Alice's Adventures in Wonderland and Through the Looking-Glass,* Oxford University Press, Oxford, 2009.

Biography

Douglas-Fairhurst, R., *The Story of Alice: Lewis Carroll and the Secret History of Wonderland,* Harvill Secker, London, 2015.

Hudson, D., *Lewis Carroll: An Illustrated Biography*, Constable, London, 1954.

Leach, K., *In the Shadow of the Dreamchild: The Myth and Reality of Lewis Carroll*, Peter Owen, London, 2009.

Thomas, D., *Lewis Carroll: A Portrait with Background*, John Murray, London, 1996.

Woolf, J., *The Mystery of Lewis Carroll: Discovering the Whimsical, Thoughtful, and Sometimes Lonely Man who created* Alice in Wonderland, St Martin's Press, New York, 2010.

Guides to Sources, Criticism

Elwyn Jones, J. and J.F. Gladstone, *The Alice Companion. A Guide to Lewis Carroll's Alice Books*, Macmillan Press, Basingstoke, 1998.

Phillips, R., *Aspects of Alice*, Penguin, Harmondsworth, 1971.

From Oxford to the World

Jaques, Z., and E. Giddens, *Lewis Carroll's* Alice's Adventures in Wonderland *and* Through the Looking-Glass: *A Publishing History,* Ashgate, Farnham, 2013.

Sigler, C. (ed.), *Alternative Alices: Visions and Revisions of Lewis Carroll's Alice Books. An Anthology*, University Press of Kentucky, Lexington, KY, 1997.

Susina, J., *The Place of Lewis Carroll in Children's Literature*, Routledge, New York and London, 2010.

Tosi, L., with P. Hunt, *The Fabulous Journeys of Alice and Pinocchio*, McFarland, Jefferson, NC, 2018.

Places

Davis, M.J., *Alice in Waterland: Lewis Carroll and the River Thames in Oxford,* Signal Books, Oxford, 2010.

Lovett, C., *Lewis Carroll's England: An Illustrated Guide for the Literary Tourist*, White Stone Publishing, London, 1998.

Specialist Topics

Lindseth, J.A, and A. Tannenbaum (eds), *Alice in a World of Wonderlands: The Translations of Lewis Carroll's Masterpiece*, Oak Knoll Press, New Castle, DE, 2015.

Lovett, C., *Lewis Carroll Among his Books: A Descriptive Catalogue*, MacFarland, Jefferson, NC, 2005.

White, L., *The Alice Books and the Contested Ground of the Natural World*, Routledge, London and New York, 2017.

Wilson, R., *Lewis Carroll in Numberland: His Fantastical Mathematical Logical Life*, Allen Lane, London, 2008.

Children's Literature

Carpenter, H., *Secret Gardens*: *A Study of the Golden Age of Children's Literature*, Unwin, London, 1987.

Carpenter, H., and M. Prichard, *The Oxford Companion to Children's Literature*, Oxford University Press, Oxford, 1984.

Darton, F.J.H., *Children's Books in England*, third edn, rev. B. Alderson, Cambridge University Press, Cambridge, 1982.

Knoepflmacher, U.L., *Ventures into Childhood: Victorians, Fairy Tales, and Femininity,* University of Chicago Press, Chicago, 1998.

Murphy, R., 'Darwin and 1860s Children's Literature: Belief, Myths, or Detritus', *Journal of Literature and Science*, 5, 2, 2012, pp. 5–21.

Novels

Thomas, D., *Belladonna: A Lewis Carroll Nightmare*, Macmillan, London, 1983.

Roiphe, K., *Still She Haunts Me*, Review, London, 2001.

PICTURE CREDITS

INDEX